DYING AND GRIEVING

Alan Billings is an Anglican parish priest in Kendal and Director of the Centre for Ethics and Religion, Lancaster University. Before that he was a priest in inner-city Sheffield – where he was Deputy Leader of the City Council – Vice Principal of Ripon College, Cuddesdon and Principal of the West Midlands Ministerial Training Course, Birmingham. He was a member of the Archbishops' Commission on Urban Priority Areas – which produced the report *Faith in the City* – and sits on the Community Cohesion Panel, set up by the Home Office following the riots in Bradford, Oldham and Burnley.

In memory of L
Time does not heal

Dying and Grieving

A Guide to Pastoral Ministry

Alan Billings

SPCK

Published in Great Britain in 2002
Society for Promoting Christian Knowledge
Holy Trinity Church
Marylebone Road
London NW1 4DU

British Library Cataloguing-in-Publication Data

A catalogue record for this book is available from the British Library

ISBN 0-281-05526-2

1 3 5 7 9 10 8 6 4 2

Typeset by Trinity Typing, Wark-on-Tweed
Printed in Great Britain by Antony Rowe Ltd, Chippenham, Wilts

Contents

Acknowledgements

These chapters began life as talks and lectures to theological students at Ripon College, Cuddesdon, the Queen's College, Birmingham, the Urban Theology Unit, Sheffield, the West Midlands Ministerial Training Course, Birmingham, and the College of the Resurrection, Mirfield; to Readers of the Dioceses of Blackburn and Carlisle; and to participants on courses at the Centre for Practical Christianity, Kendal, and the Centre for Ethics and Religion, Lancaster University. I have also been greatly helped in understanding the nature of loss in contemporary British society from conversations with Jane Smith, Hilary Binks, Teresa Onions, Brian Stabler, the Revd Jean Radley RN, Elizabeth Hawthorne and Dr Mike Howse in Kendal and members of the congregations of Walkley St Mary, Sheffield, and St George, Kendal – although they should not be held responsible for the views I express.

Prayers from *Common Worship: Pastoral Services* (Church House Publishing) are copyright © The Archbishops' Council, 2000 and are reproduced by permission.

The extract from W. B. Yeats' poem 'Death', in *The Chatto Book of Modern Poetry 1915–1955*, eds C. Day Lewis and J. Lehmann, is reproduced by permission of A. P. Watt Ltd on behalf of Michael B. Yeats.

Introduction

Although organized religion is in serious decline, most funerals in Britain continue to be conducted according to the rites of one or other of the Christian churches. Consequently, every week, priests and ministers of the different churches are in contact with the bereaved, helping them plan a funeral, talking to them about death and what it means, bringing what comfort and consolation they can, speaking about the Christian hope in sermons and addresses. In a few cases they may also have had contact with the dying. In addition, growing numbers of lay people in each of the churches are becoming involved in various forms of pastoral visiting.

This book seeks to give those engaged in or training for this ministry two things: first, some sense of how the place of religion, the nature of the funeral service and patterns of dying, mourning and grieving have changed in Britain over the past fifty years; and second, some pointers to good practice for today. It is in three parts.

Part One: Setting the scene. I begin by asking two crucial questions:

- What is the place of religion in contemporary society? (Chapter 1)
- What can Christianity say about death that might carry conviction in contemporary society? (Chapter 2)

Part Two: The changing landscape of dying, death and bereavement. I then look back over the recent past and ask what has changed in respect of

- the way we come to die (Chapter 3)
- the way we understand death and conduct funerals (Chapter 4)
- the way we mourn and grieve (Chapter 5)

and what trends we can discern.

Part Three: Improving pastoral ministry today. In the light of all of this I ask

- What is the nature of the pastoral care Christians can offer the dying? (Chapter 6)
- How should we conduct a funeral? (Chapter 7)
- What pastoral care can we offer the bereaved? (Chapter 8)

Finally I make a broad summary, in the Afterword.

At the end of most chapters I also add an account of a death with which I have been concerned at different points in my own ministry, roughly from the late 1960s, illustrating in some way points made at a more theoretical and abstract level.

But are there not already many books about dying and grieving by Christian authors? Yes and no. There are indeed many books, but they tend to be written from either a theological or a psychological perspective. Although I shall not ignore either theology or psychology, I also want to set these insights in a wider sociological and cultural setting. The reason for this is that I shall be arguing that the way we deal with death is not the result of timeless, universal psychological mechanisms but is shaped by assumptions deeply embedded in the wider culture – which change over time. I hope to draw out what some of these cultural assumptions are and how they have changed and are changing. At one time the Christian understanding of death would have been widely understood and accepted. This is no longer the case and if Christian pastors, lay or ordained, are to minister to the dying and the bereaved in the future they will need to recognize the points at which Christian assumptions and those of the wider culture are likely to diverge.

The book is arranged in such a way that after Part One, the chapters can be read sequentially, or each chapter in Part Two (which looks back over the recent past) can be followed by its parallel chapter in Part Three (which considers the contemporary situation and points to the future). So, for example, the book can be read in this way:

Chapter 1
Chapter 2

Chapter 3 followed by Chapter 6
Chapter 4 followed by Chapter 7
Chapter 5 followed by Chapter 8
Afterword

PART ONE
SETTING THE SCENE

~1~

Something happened

From traditional community to post-traditional society

I am the master of my fate:
I am the captain of my soul.
William Ernest Henley

Introduction

Something happened in the twentieth century that caused British people to change the way they thought about and responded to death.[1] Some of the most significant changes came in the period 1960–80. After that, patterns were established which have largely persisted, though there is some evidence of further development as we moved from the last century and into the early years of the present. Tracing the changes and the trends they set in motion will give us, as members of the Christian church, valuable clues as to how we may improve the pastoral care we offer to the dying, to the bereaved and to mourners both now and in the future.

Although I am aware of the many different ethnic and religious minorities which now make up British society, my concerns will centre on the majority, principally white, population.[2] There are two reasons for this. First, these are in fact the people to whom the Christian churches mainly minister. Second, and more importantly, it is only too easy for those who work with the dying and the bereaved to assume that they understand the mainstream and only need to devote time and effort to thinking about minorities. A teaching hospital in the north of England, for example, runs courses for medical staff on the beliefs and mourning rituals of a range of subgroups – Muslims, Hindus, Sikhs, and so on – but nothing on the majority culture, as if the beliefs and practices of the mainstream were not only unproblematic but also static.

This is not primarily a work of theology, although Chapter 2 deals with some theological concerns. However, it would be impossible to discuss these matters as a Christian without being theological. One reason for writing this book at all is to make it clear to those engaged in Christian pastoral ministry that the way people respond to death – their own or other people's – cannot be understood without also understanding what they believe about death. And what they believe is likely to be influenced by the assumptions of the dominant culture. Perhaps what I mean to suggest is that theology is not my main concern. There are, however, theological presumptions underlying what I say and I will try to make them clear when the need arises.

I write with two groups of people particularly in mind: the clergy and those lay people who have an involvement with the dying or the bereaved (including those training for either ministry). Many of the latter will have their ministry accredited in some way – Anglican Readers, for example. Others will be members of pastoral visiting teams or will have found themselves called upon to befriend those facing death or dealing with bereavement in their community. As the number of full-time clergy falls, the role of lay pastors increases in significance. I usually refer to the clergy as 'the minister' or 'the pastor' and make it clear when I have a wider group including lay people in mind. In order to avoid constant repetition of 'he or she' I generally opt for an inclusive 'he'.

My starting-point is the recognition that over the past century there have been important and perhaps decisive changes affecting the mainstream and their response to death. Many of these changes happened gradually over a period of time, but the period 1960–80 was undoubtedly a watershed. By the beginning of that period the National Health Service was well established, education to secondary level was universal and the nation was beginning to enjoy a period of unprecedented peace, prosperity and individual freedom. The Prime Minister had told the country in 1957 that they had 'never had it so good', and few disagreed.[3] As a result of this, new patterns of living began to be established and new attitudes formed which changed the way we died, the way we thought about death and the way we coped with it both as individuals and corporately. In sociological terms, we witnessed the final erosion of traditional communities.

The traditional community, pre-1960

Traditional communities are those in which individual and family life is lived with a much greater reference to the wider community. In a traditional community there is a shared culture of institutions, religious and moral values, ways of thinking and norms and standards of behaviour. These 'traditions' are thought to be the natural order of things and as such are authoritative; they are 'taken-for-granted' certainties.[4] There is much less room for the exercise of individual freedom in traditional communities; those who do not conform to community norms are likely to be disapproved of, stigmatized or shunned. In traditional communities people are expected to play traditional roles associated with gender and class. Lorna Sage captures the feel of this well in her memoir of life in rural Hamner in the 1940s:

> But this was a village where it seemed everybody was their vocation. They didn't just 'know their place', it was as though the place occupied them, so that they knew what they were going to be from the beginning.[5]

We should not suppose that the period of the traditional community was totally hegemonistic: people have always struggled with the demands of the tradition when it conflicted with their own desires and wants. Nor should we suppose that we could ever live making every decision and every choice in every area of life *ab initio*. Nevertheless, I think we can make some generalizations that will help us chart what happened over the last century and especially in the period after the Second World War and what some of the continuing trends might be.

The end of traditional communities, 1960–1980

The erosion of the traditional community probably began in the period following the First World War. From the 1920s we can begin to observe the growth of a more individualistic spirit; but the years of depression and then the Second World War arrested these developments for a while. When people lost their jobs they were forced to rely again on the resources of the neighbourhood community: community is largely a function of poverty. When war broke out individual ambitions had to be sacrificed for the sake of the nation and its survival. After the war, there was a period in the 1950s when people continued to invest in the traditional community. Perhaps this was due to the memory and habits of pre-war and wartime existence. Whatever it was, the traditional community reasserted itself as we can see, for example, in the pattern of churchgoing which enjoyed a brief post-war revival.[6] But from 1960 the trends are all the other way.

The erosion of the traditional community, its norms and practices, can be observed in many areas of life. The institution of marriage would be one example. When my parents were married just before the Second World War they did not question the traditional understanding of marriage which laid down what it was to be a husband and what it was to be a wife. To get married meant that you were stepping into roles that were already defined for you: they were given. As a result, many women and some men played out roles which did not suit them and blighted their lives. But when I interview couples who want to marry now, in the early years of a new century, it is clear that there are few expectations of this kind. Each couple has to work out what their respective roles are to be. Roles are no longer given but negotiated. As we move further into the new century we can already see this negotiation on the part of couples not as a once-for-all settling of the matter but only the start of a process that will continue all through their married life as their personal circumstances alter. There will be big decisions – whose career should take precedence should conflicts of interest arise? – as well as smaller, day-to-day ones – who will look after a sick child this morning when both parents work? In traditional communities the answers to these sorts of questions are presumed because they are given, they are not negotiated. Those young people who decided to live together rather than get married – at least for a time – were signalling that they did not want their relationship to be understood in those traditional terms: they would work out what it was to be and then, perhaps, get married. In Britain we can trace a fairly traditional society up to the 1950s; but after that it rapidly breaks down.

Traditional communities were eroded as people became better educated (and so aware of alternative ways of thinking and living, more critical of what was traditional and better able to articulate and express alternatives) and more prosperous (and so able to exercise greater choice in how they lived). Eyes were opened and horizons broadened. Authority shifted from 'without' – the traditions – to 'within' – each person making their own judgements and decisions. This had a long history; what we see in the later twentieth century is the assumption of attitudes by the many which were once held only by the privileged – prosperous and educated – few.

This was held to be a good thing: we came to value people who 'think for themselves' or 'take responsibility for their own lives'. These were the catchphrases of British education throughout the 1960s and 1970s. I know this is so because I was Head of Social Studies and Religious Education in a secondary school for part of this period, and these were key objectives of the curriculum.

But even where an individual continued to accept traditional authority, this was done voluntarily and not because this was the 'natural order' of things. Among the urban working classes this cultural shift coincided with post-war programmes of slum clearance in which large sections of the population moved from the inner city to outer estates. These moves served as a catalyst in breaking older attitudes and patterns of living. But the breakdown of traditional communities affected the middle as well as the working classes, and rural dwellers as much as urban.

After this time people lived lives that were more individualistic: they made choices and decisions for themselves about how they were going to live. This is not to say that their lives lacked a community dimension, as is sometimes claimed. Indeed, it is hard to know how human beings could live at all without interacting with others in forms of community. The difference was that the way we related to others was now mainly through communities that we belong to voluntarily – communities of association which we are free to join or leave – and not to the older geographical communities into which we were born or happened to live. These trends have continued and people now belong to a whole series of 'communities' which are spread over an ever-wider geographical area: people with whom we work, people we meet socially, people who are members of the clubs and societies we belong to, and so on. Moreover, new technologies – such as the mobile telephone – enable us to keep in touch with people more easily than in the past, wherever they are. The local neighbourhood and our proximate neighbours are not as significant as they once were.

The traditional family was another casualty. Families did not disappear; but they did change. Educational opportunities and not just economic necessity as in the past meant that many young people left their home district and never returned. For them, the welfare state became a surrogate carer, taking the place of the traditional family: it looked after their children and aged parents. A progressive tax system was understood as the key mechanism for sharing the financial burden of this care and for showing solidarity with those who needed help.

During the late 1960s and 1970s there were attempts to try to save or revive the traditional community. Local authorities built community centres on council estates and a new breed of professional worker began to appear – the community worker. The community worker was not a social worker; he or she was not directly concerned with the problems of individuals or families, but with the social infrastructure of a community – what made a collection of people and families into a community with a sense of mutual care and concern. The community workers found it hard going. Residents were not too willing to devote their spare time to running adventure playgrounds or coaching the boys' football team or marching on the town hall. By and large, people were only willing to think of themselves as part of a collectivity if their community faced some external threat – the closure of their local school or factory, the building of a new ring road for commuters through their part of the inner city.

The breakdown of traditional communities worried some cultural commentators – such as journalists, politicians and religious leaders. They feared that as a result of the erosion of traditional communities and in the face of a plurality of religious and moral values we lost any means of judging between alternatives. We no longer knew what to believe in or how to behave.[7] There was much talk of the need to rediscover community or find new forms of community – not for the commentators, of course, who were quite happy living their more individualistic lives, but for others. It proved elusive. People were determined to live their lives as they wanted to, being good neighbours, but only joining with others when a need arose.

Among some ethnic minorities traditional community survives, though whether this can be sustained beyond a generation or two is doubtful. The role of women – as the major influence on the next generation – is critical, and the evidence seems to be that younger women want the kind of freedom that can only come with the end of traditional families and traditional community.

Among the casualties of the erosion of traditional communities were the churches. It was not just that people stopped going to church in the 1960s, though they did in large numbers, but it was also that religion – Christianity – began to lose its privileged hold on the mind of the British people and its place in their affections. People could see clearly now that there was nothing inevitable about Christian faith or about religion. Modern British society contained within it people of many faiths and none, and the world did not fall apart. In the words of the religious sociologist Peter Berger, 'pluralism undermines the taken-for-grantedness of beliefs and values'.[8]

The institutional decline is well known and can be exemplified in two sets of figures: confirmations in the Church of England (since this represents committed membership) and attendances at Sunday school (since this shows the influence of Christian faith on a wider population.)

Table 1: Confirmations in the Church of England every twenty years, 1900–1997

1900	181,154	1960	190,71
1920	199,377	1980	97,620
1940	142,294	1997	40,881

Cited in C. Brown, *The Death of Christian Britain.* Routledge, London, 2001.

As we have noted, there was something of a mini boom in religious observance immediately after the Second World War, but from the 1960s commitment to the church in terms of confirmations fell sharply and has been declining ever since. (Similar figures for all other mainstream churches could be produced.) The most significant losses have been among the middle classes and women, especially younger, professional women. The failure of the church to hold women has had a triple effect. There was the loss of the women themselves. There was the loss of the husbands who in the past had accompanied their wife to church but out of a sense of duty rather than personal commitment; when their wives stopped attending, the men did too. Finally, as these unchurched women became mothers they no longer took their children, the next generation, to Sunday school. This was serious, since the replacement of one generation of Christians by their children is one of the most important factors in maintaining the Christian church.

Table 2: Sunday School Movement every ten years, 1901–1961: numbers enrolled and percentage of the British population

1901	5,952,431	16%	1941	3,565,786	8%
1911	6,129,496	15%	1951	3,047,794	6%
1921	5,256,052	12%	1961	2,547,026	5%
1931	4,823,666	11%			

Figures from C. Davies, 'Moralization and demoralization: a moral explanation for changes in crime, disorder and social problems', in D. Anderson (ed.), *The Loss of Virtue: Moral Confusion and Social Disorder in Britain and America.* Social Affairs Unit, London, 1992, p. 11.

The decline of the Sunday school has been particularly severe and significant. Since the late eighteenth century this had been one of the chief ways in which the church had influenced with Christian values almost every part of society. At the beginning of the twentieth century three out of every four children in the country attended Sunday school and so were exposed to Christian influence. As late as 1957, 76 per cent of people over 30 years of age had attended Sunday school at some time. But since the 1960s the Sunday school movement has all but collapsed.

This might have mattered less if religion had continued to be taught in schools. But from the 1960s, religious syllabuses in state schools began to change significantly. Generally speaking, they lost their more narrow focus on Christianity and especially the Bible. This marked an enormous cultural shift. For several hundred years the Christian church had imposed its understanding of the world on the culture of the British people. In the twentieth century that monopolistic position was undermined. Not only were fewer children coming directly under the influence of the church, but within the state education system Christianity was no longer held to be self-evidently true; in the new RE syllabuses it was taught as one religious option among many.[9] These far-reaching changes created in Britain for the first time since at least the Reformation a generation of people who were ignorant of both the scriptures and the wider Christian tradition. It led the Cardinal Archbishop of Westminster, Cormac Murphy-O'Connor, to say to his clergy in 2001 that Christianity in Britain had 'almost been vanquished'.[10]

This raises the question of what difference this is making or will make to Britain and the British in the future, or whether it will make any discernible difference at all. Christians assume that a non-Christian future must be very different from a Christian one; but this begs a lot of questions. On the one hand, we need to ask whether Christianity has simply now exhausted itself. It has left its imprint on British culture; but has it anything further to contribute as a living faith? This is not an unusual phenomenon. We continue to be influenced by Greek culture even though we no longer believe in Greek gods. On the other hand, it is equally possible that Christian values and virtues need Christian faith to sustain them and will wither without it.

The emergence of post-traditional society, after 1980

The decline of religion did not necessarily mean the disappearance of the spiritual. As the century drew towards its close it became clear that some people who believed they had a spiritual aspect to their lives felt that institutional religion could not help them and they had to turn elsewhere.[11] John Lennon and the Beatles had told people to 'imagine' a world without religion, a better world of brotherhood and love. The appeal was to fashion your own vision, your own spirituality, by exploring and enriching your own inner world, not simply adopting traditional teachings and practices. Traditional religion might be useful – as a resource. Christianity, however, being familiar, looked jaded. There seemed more promise in the unfamiliar – in Eastern religions, for example. But spiritual resources might be found anywhere, in any religion and in any writings or practices. The only test was whether they were helpful to you as you crafted your own spirituality. These exercises in constructing a personal spirituality were done without benefit of either churches or clergy, though they did produce a voluminous literature. Bookshops began to create a shelf and then a whole section devoted to 'body, mind and spirit'. All of these changes were aspects of what has come to be called the 'postmodern'. The changed attitude had been signalled well before this in a piece of Victorian poetry:

> Out of the night that covers me,
> Black as the Pit from pole to pole,
> I thank whatever gods may be
> For my unconquerable soul.
>
> In the fell clutch of circumstance,
> I have not winced or cried aloud:
> Under the bludgeoning of chance
> My head is bloody, but unbowed.
>
> Beyond this place of wrath and tears
> Looms but the Horror of the shade,
> And yet the menace of the years
> Finds, and shall find, me unafraid.
>
> It matters not how strait the gate,
> How charged with punishment the scroll,
> I am the master of my fate:
> I am the captain of my soul.[12]

Everyone came to believe they were the captain of their own soul, and whatever punishments might be charged to their scroll they would not flinch from making their own decisions and accepting the consequences. We ceased to be deferential – to institutions, to texts, to authority figures.

These are complex issues. I raise them simply to make the point that something of immense significance happened in the late twentieth century, which is still working itself out. Among other things it will affect the way we think about dying, death and bereavement.

But there were two important consequences of the collapse of organized religion, which tend to be overlooked by the church: the displacement of religion as a source of meaning in people's lives and a consequent loss of social usefulness on the part of the clergy. In traditional society religion was valued. It provided the framework in which most people thought about the meaning of their lives and their deaths. The pastoral work of the clergy, underpinned by religious assumptions they shared with parishioners, was valued: clergy were socially useful. In previous centuries their usefulness extended to many areas of life which have since become separate professions. In the eighteenth and early nineteenth centuries clergy were teachers, law enforcers, charity dispensers, welfare workers, and so on. These tasks were all stripped away with the rise of modern professions and the coming of the welfare state.[13] At the end of the twentieth century the counselling movement completed the transference of pastoral care from a religious to a secular setting. This left the clergy with far fewer meaningful pastoral tasks – and a temptation to recover social value by turning themselves into one or other of the secular pastoral callings.[14] It also made many in the general population less willing to receive the ministrations of clergy since they came at a price – the price being your soul. Increasingly, therefore, pastoring at a certain level has passed from the clergy to the laity. This includes a great deal of the care of the dying and the bereaved.

The rise of the counselling movement also gives clues about what has replaced religion as a source of meaning in the lives of many if not most people. It is symptomatic of a tendency now to find meaning increasingly in relationships. At one time people would have set the story of their individual lives in the context of the larger story of the Christian faith. This would have the effect of putting the story of an individual's life into a wider context. Family and other relationships would have been important but not necessarily the most important aspect of human life: there was also the question of God's plan for the whole of creation as well as your relationship with God – your discipleship and your eternal destiny. This was a large canvas. That has now shrunk as relationships have become centre-stage. But if meaning derives more and more from relationships, we are more and more vulnerable when those relationships are threatened. For human life is ultimately precarious and death the final threat. Unless...

Perhaps it is this 'unless' that lies behind the fact that people remain reluctant wholly to secularize the funeral. While the ministrations of the church have been shunned in most areas of life, the funeral remains a largely church (especially Anglican) preserve. There are humanist funerals, but you need to be quick off the mark if you are to avoid the local vicar. Seventy per cent of funerals in England are still taken by Anglican clergy.[15]

Summary: three periods of the twentieth century

I suggest, therefore, that we think of three periods of the late twentieth and early twenty-first centuries:

- The traditional community, pre-1960
- The end of traditional communities, 1960–1980
- The emergence of post-traditional society, after 1980

Change is organic and impossible to pin down with a precise date in this way. There are always antecedents, and change in one area of life may be more accelerated than another. But the dates are useful approximations which, if we hold them in mind, will enable us to see not only that something did indeed happen about 1960 and then again from the 1980s but also, perhaps, why it happened and what it might mean for the ministry of the church in the future.

In Part Two I will look at the way these changes had their effect on dying, death (how we make sense of it) and bereavement. Then in Part Three I will try to speak about the contemporary situation and how we might minister in it. At the end of each chapter I have included brief accounts of deaths with which I have been personally concerned during the course of my own ministry. They serve two purposes. They put some of the more abstract ideas into an actual context. They will also provoke further thought and in doing so illustrate what must become a normal part of all ministry – reflection on what we are involved with day by day. The vignettes are (edited) notes I made at the time or shortly afterwards as I struggled to make sense of what I was experiencing. I have also included some questions as a further means of provoking thought. If the book is read as part of a course of preparation for ministry to the dying or bereaved they can serve as the basis for group discussion.

Before this, however, I turn to matters of belief. What does Christianity have to say about death that will carry credibility with people in the twenty-first century?

Death in Scotland and England, 1963

This is an account of two funerals I attended in Scotland and England in 1963. The two funerals could hardly be more different and illustrate changes, which will be discussed in later chapters. The first is a description of 'traditional' death, the second of what happened as we moved away from the traditional to the 'municipal' funeral in the period of transition.

In 1963 I took a vacation job over one summer as a river watcher near to Cape Wrath in the farthest corner of north-west Scotland. I was a theological student and wanted an extended period of quietness in which I could learn some New Testament Greek. I lived in a small wooden hut on the banks of the Dionard River, a mile or two from the Kyle of Durness. My only task was to patrol the river from time to time, principally at night, to ensure that no one fished for salmon or sea trout without a permit. I worked for a landowner called Mrs Fergusson who lived in Perth but kept a hunting lodge near the river. My only companions were sheep who roamed freely across the hills and valleys, and a scattering of shepherds and their families who lived in small crofts in the surrounding countryside. The scenery is spectacular, with steep cliffs by the sea at the Cape, long, heather-covered hills and valleys, peat bogs, rivers and sea lochs.

The McDonald family, whose cottage was about a mile away from my hut, befriended me, supplying me with fresh milk from their cow, taking me with them to dig and stack peat, and, one night, to hunt down the foxes who were worrying and killing the sheep. (The killer – to their great distress – turned out to be a rogue sheepdog belonging to a neighbour.) I also met other crofting families who were members of the Presbyterian Church at Durness to which I would cycle on Sundays. They were relatively poor people who worked long, tiring hours, walking miles each day across the hills looking after the sheep and collapsing onto the leather couches they all seemed to have beside the peat stove when they returned in the evening.

One day the McDonalds' boy came to my hut bearing a message. An old woman had died and the family had invited me to her funeral. I barely knew the family but considered it a great honour to be asked to such a family occasion. I soon discovered that this was not so much a family as a community event and I was, however temporarily, a member of the community.

The woman had in fact been dying for the whole of the time I had been in the area and one Sunday after church I had gone with the McDonalds to see her. It was a long walk to her remote cottage, but each Sunday different families had taken it in turns to say their farewells. We found her in bed, propped up between two enormous white pillows, starched and stiff. She was 95 with two bright eyes and long, bony hands. She spoke freely about her coming death: it was the right time; she was tired now and ready to meet the Lord. As she said all this in an unemotional and matter-of-fact way, her two devoted daughters who fussed about looking after her, nodded their agreement. Above her bed was a small piece of framed tapestry bearing the words, 'The eye of God is over all.'

On the day of the funeral I cycled into the hills back to the cottage where she had spent all her life and in which she had died. (I learnt afterwards that the furthest the old lady had ever travelled was Inverness. She had found this such a distressing experience that she never left the valley again.) As I drew near I thought for a moment that I had made a mistake and come to the wrong place. There was a group of men – about thirty altogether – outside the cottage who from a distance looked like an assembly of freemasons or barristers waiting for the courts to open. They all wore dark clothes; some had black jackets and trousers; some carried bowler hats and furled umbrellas. At first I did not recognize them as my friends the local shepherds. There were no women to be seen and when I asked where they were Murdo McDonald explained that from the day the old woman had died no women in the vicinity had come out of their houses – as a mark of respect. Nor would they appear in public until after the body was buried.

The service was to be held in front of the house. The family were regular members of the local kirk and the elders now stood waiting by the door.

The open coffin, box-like and roughly made by one of the shepherds, was brought out and placed on two trestles. We could all see the dead woman quite plainly. Then the lid was solemnly nailed down and the service began. It was led by one of the lay elders of the church; there was no resident minister in Durness. He drew a deep breath like a man about to play the pipes, and began to chant in Gaelic what Murdo assured me was Psalm 23. Everyone else joined in as best they could. It was a mournful rendition. After the singing he read at length from 1 Corinthians 15 and then repeated what St Paul had said in his own words. Each time he made a telling point – which meant a point already made in scripture – the men would murmur their assent. The sermon then led into a lengthy prayer which assured us that the dead woman was in the hands of God and the whole service ended with another piece of Gaelic singing. I remember thinking it strange that there were no prayers for the family and nothing resembling a tribute; no attempt was made at any point to recall her life. That belonged to the past and we were there to celebrate not the past but the glorious future that awaited all of us, God willing, in heaven – if we repented and believed. That was the entire focus of the service.

As the singing died away I began to realize what might have been the real reason for my being invited: the coffin had to be carried three miles to the burial ground on the seashore at Durness, and the more hands and shoulders the better.

We formed ourselves into two parallel lines behind the coffin. Then the first four men lifted the coffin on to their shoulders and began to walk towards the seashore with the rest of us following in pairs. Every so often the little procession would stop and the next four men would move forward and take the coffin. In this way, by the time we reached the graveyard the coffin had been passed down the lines to the last group.

There was one other ritual. As well as the body, we also carried a second box. This had the liquid refreshment in. It was indeed thirsty work under a hot August sun walking the hills of Sutherlandshire, though the number of bottles of whisky we had in the box seemed somewhat excessive.

As the journey continued, the length of time between stops became shorter and the drinking time longer. The air was warm and the white and purple heather made an inviting couch. I was a source of endless amusement because I could never drink my quota of whisky at each stop. I was already feeling light-headed after the first. Murdo told me that on occasions in the past they had reached the cemetery with a crate of empty bottles and no idea where the coffin was.

The graveyard itself was on a windswept slope beside the sea. When the tide was full waves would sometimes break over the graves and the grey-white headstones nearest the water's edge. In winter it would be a bleak spot; but on this day the sun was shining and the sky was Mediterranean blue.

There were no undertakers in this part of Scotland. Having reached the cemetery we took it in turns to dig the grave. Then after further prayers the woman was laid to rest, 'dust to dust, ashes to ashes', more Gaelic psalms were sung and another little homily offered on the joys and certainties of the afterlife – for those who knew Christ. Finally, the spade was passed around for each of us to shovel earth on top of the coffin, and say a private farewell as we did so.

As I came away from this funeral I wondered whether this was one of the last places in Britain where do-it-yourself funerals were still undertaken by the community as a whole on behalf of the family. In 1963 it already had an out-of-time feel to it.

***

Two weeks after I returned from Scotland I attended the funeral of a near neighbour in Leicester.

The deceased was a relatively young, single man who had lived an uneventful life working in the final assembly department of Imperial Typewriters, a big local employer at that time. For a short period he had served in the army in Korea – perhaps the only time in his life that he had ever been given responsibility and certainly the only time that anything exciting had happened to him. He once told me that the suffering of some of his comrades in the war as well as his mother's final illness had made him a convinced atheist. His dying mirrored his life: he died alone, from cancer of the throat, on a Nightingale ward in the City General Hospital after a long and painful illness. He had smoked twenty Woodbines every day since he was 14. During the last days of his life he had no visitors apart from the medical staff who nursed him.

The service was at Gilroes, the municipal crematorium, one of the first to be built in the 1920s. There were two chapels and it was soon apparent that the timetable for the day had gone awry. One service had overrun the half-hour allocated and two sets of funeral cortèges were now waiting on the driveway for the same chapel. There were large groups of people milling about and looking bewildered since there was no indication as to which funeral was being held in which chapel and at what time.

Eventually we left the cars and followed the coffin and the duty chaplain into the building. The ceremony was perfunctory. The music was recorded; it crackled and cut off abruptly when the chaplain reached his stall. The prayer books were well thumbed and several seemed to have pages missing. The kneelers were musty.

The chaplain conducted the service at some speed, no doubt trying to make up for some of the lost time. He called our deceased neighbour by a name we did not recognize. Some mourners looked startled, momentarily wondering whether in the confusion they had wandered into the wrong funeral. At a ham tea in a local pub afterwards we discovered from his only surviving relative that this was indeed the name on his birth certificate; he had dropped it because it was the name his mother used to chastise him. The priest's use of it must have seemed like the last reprimand.

Since the chaplain did not know the deceased or the mourners there was nothing he could say in his briefest of brief addresses which was in any way personal to him or to us. We were left with the distinct impression that he had used this precise form of words many times before, and would do so many times to come.

But he did assure us that like all Christian believers the dead man was now safe in God's arms.

Twenty minutes after going into the chapel we were watching the coffin disappear across a set of bumpy rollers through a small curtained aperture towards the cremators. My father beside me thought he saw a puff of smoke, but I think it was dust from the blue velvet curtains which had probably hung there uncleaned since the building was opened.

People filed out, shaking hands with the chaplain as they left. I thought I might explain that I was an ordinand, but just before I reached him an anxious official appeared and asked him to break off and conduct a service in the chapel next door. It seemed that the minister had not turned up and the hearse was needed for another funeral.

Sic transit. Was this the best we could do?

Questions

1. What are the principal differences between the two funerals described here? Think about

   - the involvement of the community
   - the role of professionals
   - the disposal of the dead
   - the place of mourning.

2. Does it matter whether bodies are buried or cremated? Does the manner of disposal suggest anything about how people understand death?

~2~

What can we say about death?
Giving shape to experience

Teach me to live that I may dread
The grave as little as my bed.
Thomas Ken

To die should not be a verb. It's not a doing word. Death is just an absence. An absence of action; of life; of anything. An undoing word.
Alice Wignall

Introduction

One of my more uncomfortable moments as a young priest was when a very distressed, newly bereaved widow gripped my hand and asked, 'Please tell me, where is my husband now?' I was shaken not only by the intensity of the emotion but also, as we talked, by the realization that death was not something to which the woman had ever given much serious thought. We live in a culture which does not prepare people particularly well for death and which scarcely presumes life after death. But how to answer?

Until relatively recently the Christian pastor could assume that he and the bereaved shared at least the outline of a common faith. That could be taken for granted. Accordingly he would have comforted people by speaking directly and with some confidence and authority about the Christian hope. But during the course of the last century the Christian account of what it means to live and die began to lose its power; it was 'slowly coming to be doubted everywhere'.[1] In this situation it is tempting for the pastor to avoid using the Christian tradition as he seeks to make sense of the experiences of those to whom he is ministering. Tempting but mistaken, for that task – using the

Christian faith to give shape to experience – is crucially what makes pastoral ministry Christian and why people have not abandoned the religious funeral in significant numbers. If the pastor fails in this, the distinctive dimension of his care will be missing; Christian ministry is reduced to therapy and becomes another instrument of secularization.

This is not to say that the minister must talk theology every time he visits. That would be tedious for everyone. But what he says and does must be informed by Christian faith, and he must be ready to answer questions when they come. If he is to do this well he must develop for himself habits of reflecting on experience in the light of the Christian tradition. He must get into the way of having a conversation within himself between what he encounters – dying and bereaved people – how he reacts to what he encounters – his own feelings – and the gospel of hope.

But the crucial question remains: How to answer? In the relatively brief encounters that Christian ministers have with most people at the time of death, what can we say that will be helpful and carry credibility?

Before answering that question I will try to say something first about why many are now more sceptical about Christian claims. We need to understand and acknowledge that before we consider how we can speak about the Christian understanding of death in a culture which is moving away from the Christian faith.

Why scepticism?

The scepticism that many now have is in part scepticism about the Christian faith in particular and in part a wider disillusionment with any attempt to frame a world view. The doubting of Christian claims about life after death begins with a general shift in perspective about human life itself in the modern period. In that time the traditional religious account of human beings has suffered a number of hammer blows. Three in particular have been of great significance.

First, biblical assumptions about the earth as the centre of the universe (and so at the centre of God's concerns) have been challenged. Copernicus and later Galileo had already shown that to be untrue. More recent discoveries have made us realize that the galaxy itself is only one of billions. In addition, the age of the universe has turned out to be much greater than we thought – the concept of 'deep time'.[2] The religious understanding of the creation as the stage on which the human drama is played out has become harder to sustain when the earth is understood as a wayside planet in some small corner of the universe whose very existence seems almost accidental. Mark Twain expressed his scepticism this way: he said that if the Eiffel Tower represented the world's age, the skin of paint on the pinnacle-knob represented man's share of that age and anyone could see that the skin was what the tower was built for!

Then in the second place, biblical assumptions about humanity as the crown of God's creation have been called into question. Darwin showed that human beings were not the result of a single act of creation but had evolved over aeons from lower forms of life by a process of random selection and the triumph of the fittest. Humanity was chance rather than plan. This seemed a long way from the biblical account of humanity as made in the image of God.

Finally, Freud seemed to suggest that human beings were not even the rational creatures they thought they were. The human mind is nothing more than a function of a complex organism reacting according to discoverable laws.

Taken together, these three great advances in knowledge put at least a question mark against traditional Christian claims about the significance of human life.

As well as this specific scepticism about Christianity, more recently the people of western Europe have become suspicious of the very idea of a world view. This is one of a number of contemporary cultural shifts which have led some commentators to think that we are moving now into a new cultural phase altogether – the postmodern. The deep scepticism about world views – often called 'grand narratives' or 'meta-narratives' – was first articulated by the philosopher Jean-François Lyotard in the late 1970s.[3] It is now echoed by many writers who reflect on developments in post-traditional societies from the end of the twentieth century. Lyotard said that modernity was defined by belief in 'grand narratives' – like the idea of progress or the grand narratives of the different religions. This gave people a total world view, a comprehensive understanding of the world and their place in it. In Lyotard's view these grand narratives are all now incredible – which is one reason why some designate this period 'postmodern'. Although he tends to assert if rather than explain, we can see at least two reasons why he might think this.

In the first place, as we noted in the previous chapter, during the course of the twentieth century, as knowledge of the world has increased, we have come to appreciate the fact that there are many religions, many cultures and many subcultures within cultures. We have come to see that the human community is highly plural. This makes any single culture's grand narrative – even the biblical narrative – seem less plausible. We have also come to value pluralism – difference – and not see it as a problem to be overcome. We can see this change in attitude at work in relation to Christian mission. When the twentieth century began people tended to believe that their church or denomination possessed the truth about God exclusively. In the mission field the various Christian denominations were therefore highly competitive, believing that eternal destinies depended on holding the true version of the faith. Today, few Christians think that their church is the only true church or the only way to God. This is part of this wider shift in the culture towards respect for difference. If you ask people now whether we are right to evangelize native peoples and make their culture like our own they will probably say, 'No, we should respect different cultures.' Difference is now likely to be seen not as a problem to be overcome, but as something to be celebrated. Postmodernism is the articulation of this trend, but it is a trend which challenges traditional religion.

Then in the second place, the postmodernists point out that during the course of the past century we came to realize that people who believe in grand narratives have often sought to impose their understanding of the world on others by force. This has been true of secular as much as religious narratives. The Nazi grand narrative – belief in the superiority of the Aryan race and its historic mission to 'civilize' the world – led to the Second World War and the Holocaust. The Communist grand narrative – belief in the dictatorship of the proletariat and the classless society – led to the subjugation of eastern Europe and the gulags. More recently the grand narrative of Serb nationalism produced the horrors of ethnic cleansing in Kosovo, while that of militant Islamists has generated acts of global terrorism. Some would see a western grand narrative – of capitalism and liberal democracy – also striving for global hegemony. People who believe that they alone have the truth can be dangerous.

As Christians we can hardly repudiate our world view, but we have to recognize that if we are to minister to people in the twenty-first century we need to be willing to re-evaluate that world view when necessary. For example, there was little point in trying to hang on to the biblical cosmology, or the Genesis account of the creation of humans, as if they were literal truths assured for all time, for that required Christians to reject the findings of modern science. The narratives of creation are parables that express theological truths – ways of speaking about human significance. They are not alternative science. We must also recognize that the Christian world view reflects attitudes towards a range of people which we now find distasteful and even harmful: the attitude towards the Jews contained in St John's Gospel; the pre-modern understanding of human sexuality in Leviticus; the attitude towards women that runs through most of the scriptures and the writings of the church Fathers. The Christian world view perpetuates these attitudes unless care is taken to identify and repudiate them.

But while this re-evaluation is necessary it has come at a price. It has undermined confidence in other parts of the Christian message, for if Christianity has turned out to be such an unreliable guide in some important respects for living in this world, why should it be any more trustworthy with regard to the next? In other words, we have lost credibility and we shall only regain it if what we now say illuminates and resonates with people's experience again. That requires us to think deeply and with real honesty and integrity about our faith and experience.

Having made these caveats and cautions we can turn more directly to one part of the Christian world view – the meaning of what it is to die – and explore what the Christian faith might be able to contribute in this more sceptical age that will help to give shape to people's understanding and experience.

Where is my husband now?

The question, 'Where is my husband now?' leads on to many others. Are the dead anywhere? Do the dead pass straight into the presence of God? Is there a period of purgation or preparation? Are the dead resurrected altogether at the end of the age and if so, where are they in the mean time? Do earthly relationships continue as before? Are all the dead to be resurrected or only some? What can we say about heaven and hell? Those who visit the bereaved on behalf of the church will need to be alert to these sorts of issues, but they are only ever refinements of the question: Where is my husband now?

There are two issues here. The first is whether this woman's question is at all typical of the sort of issues that preoccupy those who are facing death, their own or other people's, in contemporary society. The second is whether the Christian minister can give any credible reassurance about a life beyond this one: what is the nature of the Christian hope and the basis for it?

W. B. Yeats wrote this about death:

> Nor dread nor hope attend
> A dying animal;
> A man awaits his end
> Dreading and hoping all…[4]

I am not sure that Yeats was right either about animals – at least some animals – or about people – at least people today. People dying in the twenty-first century may be anxious about the process of dying, but there is little evidence that the majority are greatly exercised with thoughts of another world. Similarly, those who grieve are not tortured with questions about heaven and hell. In this situation what is the minister to say?

As Christians we are not left to think about death in a vacuum; we have the Christian faith. Along with all other religions, Christianity has important things to say about death. But what it says needs to be put to use as one of the resources – there may be others – that can help make sense of experience. It may be the most helpful resource; it may not. Some people will turn to other resources as well as Christianity. But many are put off turning to Christian faith at all because they think of it as a bundle of beliefs that must be swallowed whole or not at all. This is a legacy of traditional society where that is exactly how it was: Christianity was ingested whole along with mother's milk. In a post-traditional society, however, where we are aware of the plurality of views on this and other issues, Christianity loses its privileged position. What it has to say will be received only in so far as it helps us to illuminate experience. It can never be a substitute for our own reflection, but it can be a significant aid to it. This is not to suggest that beliefs are all we need or all we mean by Christianity. Christianity has many resources to help us deal with death – prayer, worship, fellowship; but it does also offer resources for reflection.

Christian reflection on death moves between the raw experience of those facing death (whether their own or another's) and what the faith has to say about the kind of absence and presence of the dead that death creates.

Death as absence

There can be little doubt that the starting-point for reflection on death in Britain today has to be with death as absence. In previous ages, and perhaps in some other contemporary cultures, the reality of an unseen world of departed spirits might be a presumption. In such a society death might be interpreted as gain as much as loss – the dead may be absent here but they are present in heaven or with their ancestors in some other realm, or they are present again here, reincarnated. But in contemporary British culture death is 'just an absence'. To be dead is to cease to exist. Period. For the one who is dying it means that they must think of death in terms of the world going on without them. For the bereaved it means that there is a gap in the family and the community which can never be filled. That is part of the taken-for-grantedness of belief in Britain in the twenty-first century. The dead are absent and can only be present in the sense that we carry with us a memory of them. Anyone who wants to say something other than that does so against the grain of prevailing presumptions about what can be said plausibly.

The reason for this is that the meaning of death is no longer defined religiously but in secular, medical terms. This marks a very significant change in the language of death. When did this happen? How was this decided? Who redefined death in this way?

It has been a gradual process throughout the modern period. The French philosopher Michel Foucault has argued that in modern societies matters of great importance such as these are decided by those considered 'expert' in particular spheres. These judges of normality are present everywhere – teachers, doctors, judges, educators, social workers.[5] As far as death is concerned, gradually during the modern period, but especially since the creation of the National Health Service after the Second World War, the experts in death have become doctors – something I will say more about in the following chapter. The medicalization of the process of dying was probably the most important factor in the redefining of death.

This passing of the definition of death from the priest to the doctor is having very far-reaching consequences. The religious definition was not particularly sophisticated. You were dead when all bodily functions ceased. You were dead when you looked dead, even though your soul travelled on. Modern medicine, in alliance with modern philosophy, however, has redefined death as, 'brain dead'. To live as a human being is to be self-conscious, and self-consciousness is a function of the brain. When the brain dies the person dies. This distinction enables doctors to tell a relative that their loved one is dead (i.e. brain dead) while keeping the body alive for the purpose of organ donation. You could now seem to be alive yet be pronounced dead. I mention this not to pursue the many ethical issues that this immediately opens up but to illustrate the pastoral complexities that have arisen as the religious definition of death has given way to the medical. We have separated out two responses to death – the clinical and the personal – and sometimes find it hard to hold the two together.

The non-religious understanding of death is painful to contemplate. For the person facing their own death it means having to acknowledge that everything I mean by 'me' ceases to be. I am lost to the world – to my family, to my friends – and the world is lost to me. This is why we shrink from it. To die, says Alice Wignall, is an undoing word; and I am the one undone. Although I may take some comfort from the thought that I might 'live on' in the memory of those who knew me, a moment's reflection enables me to realize that this may not amount to very much. Death mocks everything that goes before, and 'The best is lost!' It takes time for the dying person to come to terms with that realization.

The bereaved also need time to absorb the meaning of their loss. Someone who played such a significant part in their life – a spouse, a partner, a child, a friend, a lover – is lost – for ever. Death is about absence.

Christians believe that there is more to be said about death than this. What the medical textbooks can tell us about death does not exhaust everything that can be said. But if we are to minister to the dying and the bereaved then we will need to begin by acknowledging this experience – that death means absence – and the pain and despair which in some circumstances that realization can bring. We will need to do that before we say anything else. The reason for this is that to contemplate the loss of your own life or the life of someone you love is a matter of the greatest significance. To speak about something more too quickly may seem glib, as if the reality of that absence is either not being fully acknowledged or, worse, denied. Christianity does not free us from the reality of death; Christianity frees us from its banality – from the idea that there is nothing more to be said.

Nevertheless, while acknowledging that death means significant absence, is there anything in the experience of people who live in an increasingly post-religious culture that gives us a way into speaking about something more? I believe there may be on some occasions, for sometimes bereaved people will say that they find the secular account of death unsatisfactory; they are left with what we might call an existential niggle that full justice is not being done to what they are experiencing.

For example, many secular accounts seek to show that death is part of the 'natural' order of things: all creatures are born, live, grow old and die. Human beings are no different from the animals in this respect. In fact, the only difference is that we live on in the memories of those who knew us. Once you acknowledge this, the argument goes, you can approach death with a calm mind: there is no more reason for a person being upset than for an animal.

This is where the niggle comes in, for this understanding of death as 'natural' strikes some bereaved people as a reduction of death as they are actually experiencing it. It does not account for the fact that in the face of death we are generally anything but calm. We rage against the dying of the light.[6] It does not seem 'natural' but a violation. It is surely a puzzle that if we are, like the animals, part of the natural creation and there is nothing more to be said about us, we have been left so unprepared to face biological death. Unless…

Death as presence – elsewhere

Unless that is, death is not to be regarded as the last word on human life. This does not necessarily make the death of a loved one any more bearable or less sad, but it does mean that we have to think about it from an altered perspective. That perspective, Christians would argue, is the perspective of faith – in the God of the Bible – for belief in an afterlife is founded on belief in God, his nature and purposes. It is because we believe that God created us to enjoy his friendship and that he is the God of the living, not of the dead, that we believe in the possibility of a renewed presence of the dead after death. God will not leave us in death.

The question for Christians today is not whether some absolute proof of life after death can be offered – such proof is simply not available – but whether speaking about life after death can be done in ways that are credible in the light of contemporary knowledge about the world and human life. Scepticism about the plausibility of claims for life after death begins, as we have already seen, with a general shift in perspective about human life itself in the modern period. Modern science (as well as philosophy) tends to suggest that although human beings may be more complex, there is no reason for thinking of them as different from other packages of matter in the universe which come into existence and pass out of existence all the time. While thoughts and feelings may not be entirely reducible to electrical activities in the brain, they are nevertheless dependent on those activities. If we think away brains and bodies we think away thoughts and feelings: thoughts and feelings cannot exist disembodied, like the smile on the Cheshire cat. In other words, when the body dies, so does whatever we mean by 'me' or 'the soul'.

If therefore the person – 'me', 'my soul' – is to exist in some other realm it needs some form of materiality to make this possible. This is precisely what the idea of the resurrection of the body, or, more accurately, the reconstitution of the person, is asserting. We are not talking here about the resuscitation of a corpse in this world or the transformation of flesh and blood, but the remaking of persons in another realm beyond physical death. This resurrection body – Paul's spiritual body – is so constituted that we are recognizable to ourselves and to those who knew us during our earthly existence. What enables us to speak of this resurrection body as 'me' is continuity of memory and the sense of personal identity. The resurrected person is able to recall their earthly existence, perhaps in some detail, and recognize some of those who had been significant in their life. If there is life hereafter it must consist in God refashioning us in some bodily form. This is why Christianity prefers to speak of resurrection rather than immortality of the soul.

However, Christians should be cautious about introducing the idea of life after death into their conversations with the dying or the bereaved and only do so in the gentlest of fashions. The reason for this is very simple: in this culture it is entirely possible that people may not have thought greatly about life after death – at least not as a serious possibility for them or for a loved one. The idea of the dead being present somewhere else can be as disturbing as the thought of them being absent here. If it takes time for people to deal with the reality of absence, it will take time for them to deal with the possibility of a renewed presence elsewhere. If the bereaved disciples, who were predisposed to believe in resurrection, took so long to accept the reality of Christ's resurrection, we should not be surprised to find bereaved people in a more secular culture needing time to change their perspective.

But rather than speaking of a life hereafter, should we not begin with the idea of resurrection and the resurrection of Christ? There is good reason for being cautious here too. In a culture that has moved a long way from the Christian tradition, the concept of resurrection is easily misunderstood. Our resurrection is not like the instances of resurrection we read about in the New Testament. It is not like the resurrection of Lazarus or the widow's son at Nain.[7] They are about the resuscitation of corpses and their return to earthly existence; Lazarus and the widow's son are raised only to die again. Nor is our resurrection like the resurrection of Jesus. His human body is not resuscitated and returned to earthly existence; it is transformed, no longer subject to this world of time and space, yet for a while visible within it. The general resurrection on the last day is about the recreation in another realm of existence of the person who once lived in this world and died. This has nothing to do with flesh and blood, for flesh and blood cannot inherit the kingdom of God. In our brief conversations with the bereaved the language of life after death is likely to be initially more fruitful.

The point we need to concentrate on in our conversation is this: if we are to live beyond death then that is to be understood as something that comes about as a result of God's goodness towards us and not as a result of some attribute of human nature. God is the God of the living not the dead, not because we are immortal but because he chooses to bestow immortality upon us, to raise us. (This suggests we might be on surer ground if we stop using the language of 'soul', or only use it with extreme care, perhaps eschewing the term 'immortal soul'.) The answer to the question, 'Where is my husband now?', therefore, is quite simply this: He is safe with God because God made him for himself. Beyond that there is little more that we either can or should add.[8]

While we should be very circumspect in what we say about the nature of the resurrection life, perhaps Jesus gave us an important clue when he said in a passage in Matthew's Gospel that in the resurrection 'they neither marry nor are given in marriage'.[9] It is perhaps the natural tendency of bereaved people to want earthly relationships restored in heaven, especially those that have been close and meaningful, such as a happy marriage. Heaven is often popularly understood in precisely this way as little more than a family reunion. The New Testament does not encourage this type of thinking, and these words of Jesus suggest why. One of the hard lessons that the disciples had to learn was that there was nothing absolute about their relationship with Jesus in the days of his flesh: it would not continue after the resurrection; Mary could not 'cling' to Jesus.[10] The disciples had to learn to relate to Jesus differently. What they had before was not lost or of no value; but they had now outgrown it and it was no longer appropriate. Similarly, we shall have to give up our loved ones in death (absence) and in heaven find them again (presence), but in a different and more wonderful relationship. This is hard to grasp. Is there anything in this life which might serve as an analogy or give us a clue as to how a special relationship might be outgrown but not lost? In a little book about marriage, the English theologian Helen Oppenheimer speaks about this text from Matthew and offers a suggestive analogy from family life. She writes:

> Being a mother or a father, in one sense, is a temporary role. In another sense, one's parents are one's parents forever. The special character of the friendship that can develop between grown-up people who have been children and parents is sometimes one of the most rewarding aspects of human life. At its best it is enhanced by plenty of happy memories, but it does not have to live on memories: it is a going concern.[11]

The New Testament may see marriage and the family as important relationships, but it does not absolutize them either in this world or in the next because this world and its concerns have to be given up in death – 'Do not cling...'

Finally, whatever more we say about the life of the world to come has to be recognized as inevitably symbolic language. We seek to convey truths by means of analogies and pictures. So the resurrection of the dead means that all that I mean by 'me' is reconstituted by God after death; and because I cannot conceive of a disembodied me, this must mean that I have in some sense a body, as St Paul recognized. Similarly, notions such as purgatory, judgement, heaven and hell are pictures which seek to convey truths. Judgement suggests that the way we live on earth matters, not least because what we have made of ourselves by our earthly choices will have to be dealt with if we are to live happily in heaven. Purgatory hints at the possibility of development and growth in the hereafter. Heaven points to the possibility of bringing our potential to full fruition. Hell should be reinterpreted to mean not everlasting punishment – a view which most Christians had abandoned by the beginning of the last century – but the fact that choices made in the here and now leave their mark on our character and will have to be accounted for. Moreover, the suggestion is that all who are brought to judgement will experience their moment of hell – facing the full truth – before they can know heaven.

Where is my husband now? – the question with which we began. Looked at from the perspective of this world, the dead are dead, absent; they 'exist' only in the mind of God who holds the 'blueprint', the template, of each individual until that moment when he shall resurrect them, make them present again. From the perspective of heaven, which is beyond this realm of space and time, we have all run our course and are raised together, judged and brought into God's nearer presence. In the hereafter it is already the end of the age.

Preaching at funerals

Those who preach at funerals need to bear in mind how diverse the contemporary congregation is going to be. There will be those who accept traditional Christian teaching. There will be those who have some alternative understanding of death – as the end of life, as the gateway to a new incarnation. But there will be a third group, who may well be the majority, who have no settled opinion, who are still searching. They want to hear something of the Christian gospel, but expressed in a manner which invites them to consider rather than suggests to them that there is only one way of approaching the matter. In contemporary culture the one thing everyone knows is that there are alternatives.

Those most closely affected by the death may well be in no state to concentrate on what the minister says about the gospel at all, however eloquent or cogent the preaching. This is not to say that nothing will be communicated. On the contrary, both the liturgy itself and the way in which the minister conducts the whole service will speak to them about the Christian hope in the face of death. But there is always that group of people who are touched by this death yet are not in such emotional turmoil that they cannot take in what the preacher is saying. In fact, they may well be very reflective in the face of death and receptive to thoughtful explication. We fail to minister to them if we do not make some attempt to say something, however succinct, about the Christian perspective: death is not the last word on anyone's life; God cares for us in life and in death; in his nearer presence we shall know ourselves again.[12]

Conclusion

In Europe there has been a waning of interest in religion during the past fifty years and a shift in attitudes towards death. Even where people have a lively interest in religion the dominant concerns are not with the next world but with living this one to the full.[13] Whereas at one time death was feared and regarded as 'unnatural' because it struck when people were in the prime of their lives, today, because of a greater life expectancy, its visitation may seem more like a blessed release and the 'natural' climax of a fulfilled life. People who reach these advanced years often say that they are 'ready to die' or 'tired now' – suggesting that their life has reached a satisfactory conclusion. The idea that it might continue in another realm is not as attractive as it might have been in previous eras when life was so often cut short by disease, war or accident. The test of religion by many in the contemporary world, however, is not whether it guarantees my life after death but whether it helps me to live better before I die. It is not surprising, then, that people want the focus of the funeral service to be on the quality of a life lived rather than a life to come. This does not mean we should say nothing; but it does suggest that we need not say quite as much as we did.

Questions

1. 'May the souls of the faithful departed, through the mercy of God, rest in peace.' How would you explain this to an enquirer?
2. Are people today more afraid of the process of dying than anything that might happen afterwards? Does this matter?
3. 'Reunited' – it says on the gravestone of a married couple. How true is this likely to be?
4. Can there be Christianity without belief in personal resurrection?

PART TWO

THE CHANGING LANDSCAPE OF DYING, DEATH AND BEREAVEMENT

-3-

Dying
The way we die now

Life, then, may be delightful, a playground or even a paradise, but it has a price tag attached to it: no one gets out of it alive.
H. M. Kuitert

Alone into the Alone.
C. S. Lewis, *A Grief Observed*

He just stood and looked at his dying mother, his heart too full for words.
William Faulkner, *As I Lay Dying*

Introduction

Dying is something we do for ourselves; we cannot ask someone to die on our behalf. Perhaps it is more accurate to say that dying is not something we do but something done to us since we cannot by some act of will postpone the event or choose some alternative: it is inescapable, and it is into the unknown. Having said that, all other generalizations are only more or less true. Nevertheless, as we look back over the last century and the early years of this we can discern some significant changes in the way most people came to their deaths. In this chapter I will plot something of how, where, when and why people died. In the following chapter I will consider the funeral and the question of how death was interpreted and understood, and then in Chapter 5 I will turn to changes in the patterns of grieving and mourning. So these three chapters are about dying, death and bereavement and significant changes over the course of the last century and this. Understanding those changes and what they suggest about the changing context in which we come to die will help us to develop our ministry to the dying and the bereaved in ways that are both sensitive and appropriate. They may also stimulate us into thinking about our own death and how we might prepare ourselves for it.

The traditional community, pre-1960

'In life we are in the midst of death' is a text which would have resonated with all people at the beginning of the twentieth century. The words are from the Burial Service of the Book of Common Prayer and were spoken by the priest as the coffin was lowered into the grave. They accurately reflected the fragility and uncertainty of life for most people in the period before the creation of the National Health Service. Life was a lottery. In large part your chances of living a long life were dependent on the social class into which you were born and the occupation you followed. For the majority, medical care was poor and life was short. But life was uncertain for people in all social classes because illnesses were not always treatable. Death could strike without warning and at any age.

This had in fact been true for most of British history. Life was nasty, brutish and short, and death was an ever-present reality, suddenly devastating individual families and even whole communities. The records of those times are all around us. When I was a vicar in Sheffield I lived near to the soot-stained monument set up in the nineteenth century to commemorate those who died in the cholera outbreaks. In the municipal graveyard nearby lay the bodies of any number of people whose lives were cut short by untreatable disease or the all-too-common industrial accidents associated with making steel and grinding blades. (Grinding wheels frequently broke as operators sharpened blades, maiming or killing the grinder who sat astride them.) One of the local churches possessed an eighteenth-century register which recorded infant baptisms at the front and infant burials at the back – for most children were dead within a year of their christening. One could see why the helpless parents chose to name their babies Mercy or Pity, though Providence or fate showed little of either.

At the beginning of the twentieth century, people died at home, not in hospitals or other institutions, though the mentally ill were likely to be institutionalized. The church had taught for generations that a good death was to die in the full knowledge that you were dying, after having made peace with God and your neighbour. People who knew they were dying, therefore, and those who cared for them, would understand 'dying well' from a religious perspective and seek to prepare for it accordingly. For Protestants this would mean acknowledging past sins in private prayer, possibly with the aid of a minister. For Catholics, both Anglican and Roman, it would require you to make a formal confession and to receive the sacrament. A few years before she died in 1901, Queen Victoria wrote in her will what is in effect a summary of the way Christians would ideally prepare themselves for death and the hope they entertained for life beyond the grave:

> I die in peace with all, fully aware of my many faults, relying with confidence on the love, mercy and goodness of my Heavenly Father and His Blessed Son and earnestly trusting to be reunited to my beloved husband, my dearest Mother, my loved Children and 3 dear sons-in-law. And all who have been very near and dear to me on earth. Also I hope to meet those who have so faithfully and so devotedly served me, especially good John Brown and good Annie Macdonald.[1]

While preparing for death did not preoccupy the twentieth-century Christian quite as much as the Victorian, let alone the medieval Christian, nevertheless, death had to be prepared for since there would be a calling to account and a determining of eternal destinies.[2] Christ might be a merciful judge, but there would be a judgement, after which souls would be separated from one another as sheep were separated from goats, some to enjoy the unspeakable bliss of heaven and others to endure the agonizing pains of hell.

But dying well was threatened on two counts. First, there might be little or no time to prepare. The typical death in the first half of the century was that of my father's sister who caught diphtheria as a teenager in the 1920s and died within days. Then in the second place, dying could be painful. Medicines, if there were any, and doctors were beyond many people's means. It was hard to approach your end with charitable thoughts towards your neighbour and love in your heart for God if your body was racked with pain. With its customary realism the Prayer Book recognized this and required the priest to say at every burial 'suffer us not, at our last hour, for any pains of death, to fall from thee'.

Throughout this period – the first half of the last century – when the dying were mainly cared for at home, death was in the hands of the family and local community, as it had been in all previous centuries. If someone were dying, the family looked after them with support from the neighbours. Neighbours might visit the dying; they would certainly offer the equivalent of 'respite care' to the relatives, sitting with the dying while wife or husband took a break or had some sleep. When someone died, they died with members of their family around them. We have a description by Archbishop Randall Davidson of Queen Victoria's bedroom as she lay dying in 1901. Although it was more crowded than most bedrooms would be, the principle of the family gathered round was not at all unusual:

> The Family were assembling, some of them not fully dressed. They knelt round the bed, the Prince of Wales on the Queen's right, the German Emperor on her left. About 10 or 12 others were there. The Queen was breathing with difficulty and moving somewhat restlessly, the nurse was kneeling behind her in the bed, holding up the pillows...[3]

After death, in many working-class districts, neighbours would help the family to wash and dress the dead prior to the undertaker arriving. Dying and death were familiar.

Until the watershed years – 1960–80 – the clergy might well be involved at various points with the dying and the dead. Clergy might be asked to prepare the dying for their death, by praying for them or anointing them (last rites). An older generation of people came to regard the visit of the clergy as a clear sign that the end was near, and this was not always welcome! The most unsuccessful clergyman of this time was surely Queen Victoria's local priest on the Isle of Wight, the vicar of Whippingham, who went to the lavatory and missed the moment of her death.[4]

Until the period of the NHS, the role of the medical profession was much more restricted. Most of my forebears in the late nineteenth and early twentieth centuries seem to have died in their own beds with only an occasional visit from a doctor – if one visited at all. The carers were the family – though sometimes certain neighbours who seemed to have developed a specialism in the care of the sick and dying. When death occurred it was the practice until well into the last century for bodies to be washed and dressed by the family or neighbours prior to removal by the undertaker. The body would then be brought back to the house, often in an open coffin, until the day of the funeral. Roman Catholic and some Anglican clergy would receive the body overnight in the church or say prayers with the family beside the body at the house the night before the funeral, and they would be consulted carefully about the form of the service, the choice of hymns and readings. But it was not until the second half of the century that care of the dying and the dead was almost wholly professionalized.

The end of traditional communities, 1960–1980

During the second half of the last century all this was to change. The most significant factor affecting the way we died was the creation after the Second World War of a government-funded welfare state within a peaceful and prospering economy. Better diets, improved housing, shorter working hours with safer working conditions, more holidays and greater access to good health care all contributed towards people living healthier, more fulfilled and longer lives. Industrial deaths, sudden deaths and the death of children became rarer as people looked forward to extended periods of retirement. All these were important gains and resulted in a gradual shift over the century from death being an ever-present possibility throughout people's lives – something which always lay in wait and struck unpredictably – to a concern in older age. Grieving was now for a life lived, not a life not lived.

Although the welfare state reduced child mortality and enabled us to live longer there was another side to the coin. As the economy changed and people became more prosperous, patterns of living began to be transformed as well. Young couples, who at one time might have married and continued living with their parents in the same house or the same neighbourhood all their lives, began to move away. This helped to accelerate the breaking-up of the relatively close-knit and stable communities which marked both inner city and outer suburb in the first half of the twentieth century. By the 1960s parents were beginning to realize that their children might live and work anywhere in the country. By the 1980s they realized it might be anywhere in the world. It could no longer be assumed that children would be on hand to look after elderly parents even if they wanted to. In addition, as the traditional community gave way to more atomized lifestyles, it became unrealistic to assume that good neighbours would be on hand in any significant way to care for the elderly either. By the end of the twentieth century only 25 per cent of the population died at home; 54 per cent died in hospital, 18 per cent in residential homes and 4 per cent in hospices.[5]

The typical death by the 1980s was death from cancer after lengthy treatment in older age.[6] In other words, death – other than by accident – was conquered in the earlier years of life and people were now dying because bodies, like all created things, eventually wear out; degenerative diseases such as cancer and heart disease now caused death. This has had a number of consequences. On the one hand, death came to be associated with old age. Anyone who died before advanced older age was thought to have been cheated in some way. What was at one time commonplace – the death of a child – now became rare and so an occasion for deep distress. For a while, there was even a virtual denial of death altogether: to admit that people died seemed to mock all the advances that were being made in medicine.[7] On the other hand, very old people ceased to be unusual and so ceased to be venerated. In both respects this was quite unlike all other periods in human history. In addition, since people died after months or years of illnesses such as cancer, they knew – or could know – for longer periods that they were terminally ill.

As people lived longer, they became more dependent on the medical profession rather than their families and tended to spend their final days in a council-run nursing home and then in hospital. It was here, in some anonymous ward, surrounded by strangers, rather than at home among family and friends, that people now died. This was a new development. Although institutional care enabled the elderly to be looked after, and in that sense helped families cope, it also put families under pressure since they had to journey to distant hospitals to visit. But it was a while before hospitals changed to meet the demands put on them. It is probably true to say that for much of the period 1960–80 hospitals were run for the convenience of staff rather than patients or their families and friends. Visiting times were restricted and sometimes the numbers of visitors as well. Rules were enforced with little understanding of the needs of either the patient or the visitor. They were depressing places and I have distressing memories from this period of visiting elderly people in homes and geriatric wards, seeing them, in Alan Bennett's telling phrase, 'shuffling the dominoes, gazing vacantly at a plate of mince'.[8]

All of this contributed to the feeling on the part of both the younger generation and the elderly themselves that old age was a burden and old people were a nuisance. 'Old' was invariably used negatively: 'interfering old…', 'boring old…', 'silly old…', 'dirty old…' This too was new. Little wonder that many people came to believe at this time that 'a good death' was dropping dead in the street or just not waking up one morning. Little wonder that relatives often – and sometimes guiltily – experienced the death of their loved ones after months of visiting a geriatric ward as a relief.

All of these changes had a considerable effect on people's experi-ence and knowledge of dying and death. As the care of the dying became more institutionalized, knowledge of dying passed to the medical profession and was lost within families and the community. Similarly, after death, the preparation of the body became exclusively the concern of the funeral director. Families might not see their dead and the dead might not be brought back to the family home.[9] Death became unfamiliar and knowledge of dying and death was lost. The historian Philippe Ariès, who has written extensively on death in Western society, spoke of dying becoming 'hidden' or 'invisible' in the twentieth century. Relegated to the side ward of an anonymous hospital, death ceased to be public with the result that 'everything goes on as if nobody died any more'.[10]

As people began to die in hospitals and away from their homes, the involvement of the clergy with the dying declined rapidly. Some urban clergy might never, or very rarely, minister to dying people during the whole of their ministry. Apart from the funeral of church members or a funeral in church arranged through the minister, the role of the clergy was restricted to the service itself. Until the last decades of the century in many urban areas Anglican clergy were on a rota at the crematorium, taking services every half-hour throughout the week. It was simply not practicable to contact mourners before the service other than by telephone, and in the 1960s few working-class families had one. Older generations may have memories of poor and impersonal services at crematoria dating from this period. It was a low-water mark for all the churches but especially the Church of England, which conducted the majority of funerals.

This period, then, marks a time when as far as the majority of people were concerned, the clergy ceased to have any involvement with the dying and the dead. They were no longer regarded as the 'experts' in death or the care of the dying or bereaved. Expertise lay with the medical profession. Clergy were rarely asked to visit the dying in hospital (except members of their own churches – and not always then) and follow-up visits to the bereaved after funerals were not always practical or welcomed.

One major consequence of the hospitalization of the majority of dying people was that dying and death were increasingly understood from a secular, clinical perspective. To die well, therefore, was about dying with minimal pain and discomfort rather than making your peace with God and neighbour. This period brought about the end of the religious death.

The emergence of post-traditional society, after 1980

Although what I have described above has remained broadly the situation since that time, there have been some further developments since the 1980s in some significant respects. Perhaps the first and most obvious point is that in our post-traditional culture, while we can still speak in broad generalities about death and bereavement, there is much more scope for individuals and families to act differently from the mainstream. This is now an increasingly plural culture which allows for and tolerates difference in a way which neither traditional Britain nor Britain in the watershed period, 1960–80, did. As the new century progresses we can expect this trend towards difference and diversity to continue. We live now in a post-traditional world.

A glance down the obituary column of a local newspaper or the list of funerals at a crematorium soon establishes that people are living even longer and many people are dying in quite advanced old age. There is no reason to suppose that this pattern will not be maintained, and every reason to believe that the number of very old people as a proportion of the population will continue to rise. Over the past two hundred years life expectancy has more than doubled: in 2000 it was 75 for men and 80 for women. It is also increasing by about two years every decade, with those over 85 being the fastest-growing segment.[11]

Although it remains the case that the vast majority of people continue to die in hospitals or nursing homes (which tend now to be private rather than municipal), more are choosing to die in their own homes. There is probably now a presumption on the part of most people in the medical, therapeutic and nursing professions that, whenever possible, people should be helped to die at home rather than in an institution. This is a trend that has been stimulated and enabled by the hospice movement. In recent years hospices have been at the forefront of helping very ill people to return to their own homes with hospice staff supporting families and friends in caring for them. There is also a national pressure group, the Natural Death Centre, which seeks to promote the care of the dying at home so that families may be involved.[12] We can expect these trends to continue. This suggests that new areas of sensitive pastoral ministry to the dying and to those who look after them might increasingly open up in the future away from hospitals.

At the same time, those who care for the dying, whether professionally or as family and friends, are much more open than they once were about both diagnosis and prognosis. There was a time, roughly from the point that the NHS came into being, when those involved with the dying were not always as frank as they might be with patients; families also tended to collude with doctors and nurses. This was justified on the grounds that it enabled the terminally ill to enjoy their last days without the extra anxiety of knowing that they had only a short time to live. In retrospect it looks as if the carers were sometimes more concerned about their own feelings and ability to cope than those of the dying. It is hard to acknowledge that a loved one is dying. It is even harder to share the knowledge with them and to know that you are going to survive and they are not. But the general disposition of people now seems to be towards telling the truth. Consequently, more people are likely to know that they are dying and to want to prepare in some way.

As some people began to take control of their own deaths again and to die at home, and as families learnt to care for the dying, knowledge of death once more ceased to be the exclusive preserve of the professionals. During the final decades of the twentieth century a large number of books, articles and poems was written and television programmes were produced in which people spoke, often very movingly, of their own experiences in facing the prospect of either their own death or that of a loved one.[13] Once again, the possibility of a life beyond this one could be openly talked about, though not necessarily in conventionally religious terms. Some popular films had death and what might follow as a major theme – *Truly, Madly, Deeply, Ghost* – though the culture was generally agnostic or even sceptical about life beyond the grave. Death itself, however, ceased to be the forbidden topic. (That became religion!) Death also ceased to be something to be afraid of. In my experience people now are much less fearful of death than they were in the 1960–80 period – though they have anxieties about the control of pain and the reactions of loved ones.

While much that has appeared in the media has been helpful, we need to be a little more cautious about the role of television. The intimacy of the 'fly on the wall' documentary can be very misleading: we can only too easily think that because we have seen a person die on television we know what it is to be in the presence of death. The reality may surprise us.

However, the greater openness about death and the willingness of many to talk about dying combined with studies of dying patients – such as those of Dr Elisabeth Kübler-Ross – is enabling us to understand the conflicting emotions of those who are consciously facing their end.[14] They may begin with anger and denial – the frantic requests for further X-rays or second opinions. They may seek to bargain. They may experience periods of profound depression and melancholy. They may be quite euphoric. They may be calm and rational or frenzied and irrational.

They may be any or all or none of these, in this or any other order. At any rate, death is no longer psychologically repressed – though it remains very private – and families are learning to recognize changing emotions and how to respond to them.

If the trend towards people taking back control of death continues, however, there may be further developments. For example, some people have already decided to do away with a professional undertaker, preferring instead to have their relatives or friends take care of them when they die. While this may be an extreme example it is indicative of the fact that people in the future will want to play a greater role in preparing for death and planning funerals.

If the trend towards people dying at home rather than in hospital continues, clergy or lay visitors may begin to develop again pastoral roles with the dying – and with people who will eventually be bereaved. The ministry of lay people may be easier to develop because it may be more easily accepted. The tradition of clergy visiting the dying has almost completely disappeared; there is only a distant residual memory of it. In any case, as religion has ceased to play a significant part in the lives of most people, the demand for the ministrations of the clergy has sharply declined. As the religious meaning of death has been abandoned, there has been a shift away from preparing people for life beyond the grave towards ensuring that the quality of their remaining years or months is as good as it can be. There may be a spiritual dimension to this even if it is not religious in the traditional sense. But in so far as clergy are asked to call, people are more likely to want them to call in the way that a good friend might – willing to share their own thoughts and doubts and feelings – rather than as a more detached professional or expert on 'religion'.

After the watershed decades a new professional appeared: the counsellor. They stepped into a vacuum created by the declining influence of the clergy and the inability of the medical profession to give patients and their families the time they needed to talk about the emotional turmoils which terminal illness, the approach of death and bereavement brings. There was a brief time – in the 1980s and early 1990s – when the counselling movement sometimes became unnecessarily prescriptive. Counsellors formulated their own psychological version of a 'good death'. This was the idea that a dying person could only come to terms with the prospect of their death by passing through certain 'stages' – to calm acceptance by way of anger and depression. This is still an influential model. However, in general there is now a realization that while the so-called 'stages' may be useful pointers to people's moods and states of minds, dying people do not necessarily pass through stages in any neat, sequential way, and people come to terms with their dying in different ways. Some take the knowledge of their dying in their stride from the beginning. Others never do. Religious commitment can play a significant part, shaping responses, though we cannot always predict how any particular person will in fact react.

Unlike the clergy, counsellors passed no judgement and had no obvious ideological axe to grind; the goal of counselling was to enable each individual to reach his or her own understanding of life and death. At the moment, counsellors are more likely to be involved with the bereaved than the dying, but the assumptions of counselling are likely to be widely shared, in particular a more psychological understanding of the good death. I will return to this in the next chapter, but for the moment we may note that such an understanding, while not incompatible with religion, does not assume a religious dimension.

The growth of the counselling movement has been steady and continuous and is found at a number of levels. There are well-qualified and experienced therapists who see themselves as professionals doing a professional job and working to professional standards and codes of conduct. But there is also a growing army of people who offer counselling in various guises, who may or may not have received any training, but who know something of counselling techniques and general approach. Much of this is at the level of simply being a 'good listener' combined with a little applied wisdom drawn from personal experience. Perhaps this is one way of genuinely returning caring to the community. Some clergy have seen it as a way for them to find an acceptable role after the collapse of a more traditional pastoral role with the dying and bereaved. It is, however, the evident humanity of the clergy or lay visitor that is valued rather than any expertise, for in the post-traditional world there are no experts, not even in death.

Summary

Let me summarize what I have said so far. I have charted some of the changes that have taken place with respect to dying over the past fifty or so years. I suggested that the watershed for these changes was the period 1960–80, during which time Britain moved from being a traditional to a non-traditional society and most people died in hospital rather than at home. That period of transition was one of confusion and muddle as we sought to understand and come to terms with the changes that were taking place. It was a particularly difficult period for the church as it lost its traditional influence and role and struggled to find others. In the new century there is some evidence that people are wanting to take more control over the way they approach their own death. Christians need to understand this and consider what the implications might be for pastoral care. For ministry in the post-traditional world will be about sharing one's experience and vulnerability, not about claiming particular expertise. The days have gone when the church could determine what spiritual resources were appropriate for the dying and control the circumstances in which they would be offered.

Dying in our street

In this account of death in a traditional working-class community in the 1950s, I recall how dying happened at home. In our street, my mother was called upon to 'lay out' the body prior to the undertaker arriving. Death was an event affecting the whole community and not simply the family.

Among my earliest memories are those of dead bodies. This is because my mother was a street 'layer out' who took me with her whenever she was called to 'lay out' the newly dead. In those years immediately after the Second World War, it was still the custom in working-class communities to prepare the body at home before sending for the undertaker. As soon as the doctor had certified the death my mother would help our neighbours put a fresh sheet on the bed (old people always had one ironed and ready for this purpose in a chest of drawers), clean and wash their loved ones, close their eyes, comb their hair, put their teeth back in their mouth and then dress them in a freshly ironed pair of pyjamas or nightdress (which were also kept ready in the chest of drawers). Only then would they be considered fit to pass into the hands of the undertaker.

My mother would already be familiar with the house because when someone was dying she would visit along with other neighbours. We would crowd into the bedroom and talk with or in front of the person dying with no particular inhibitions. Occasionally someone would say, 'Be quiet! Mabel (the one dying) wants to say something.' It was important to listen and to have witnesses because the dying person might well decide at this point which of her neighbours should get what from her possessions – a small brooch, a chiming clock, some porcelain plates in the china cabinet. Very few people made a will.

In this way, many of our neighbours prepared for their death. Distant relatives might be sent for. Sons and daughters who had been alienated might suddenly appear in the street and tearful reconciliations would follow. Occasionally this required the visit of the solicitor to change a will – a cause of instant gossip and rumour up and down the street: what could she possibly have that was worth a solicitor's visit?...

While mother worked on the body I played around the bed. It never crossed my young mind that there was anything strange about this. I didn't find the sight of a dead person especially distressing and one old person's gaunt wax-grey face seemed very much like another. Looking back, I must have been shielded from anything that might cause upset. I have no recollection of a dead child or baby, for example – yet there must have been many in those years. Nor was the smell of the room ever particularly offensive. On the contrary, I only recall now the fragrance of flowers and the strong smell of carbolic soap which mother always took with her. There was one unfortunate occasion when I crawled under a bed and encountered a rather full, days-old chamber pot, grey-green with mould, but it was quickly whisked away. I grew up, therefore, with no particular fear of the dead. It was some years before I read Tolstoy's account of the death of his mother and the piercing shriek of horror from the peasant girl when she saw the dead woman in her open coffin, and I realized that for some the sight of a dead person could be a cause of extreme distress and dread.[15]

I quite enjoyed these expeditions to other people's houses. They provided me with a chance to poke around in dark corners and discover all kinds of small objects, some of which I was allowed to take home. In this way I acquired two of my proudest early possessions: a set of bones from an old man who had whiled away his remaining years tapping out the rhythm of well-known tunes on spoons and these strips of animal bone, and some sticks of red sealing wax. The wax was in common use until the 1950s. It was melted over a candle flame and dripped like a splash of blood onto the back of an envelope or the string of a parcel to make it secure. I loved it for its deep red colour.

If I thought about death at all as a young child, I must have thought that it was something that happened to other families and only in extreme old age. This changed abruptly when I was nine. I had been taken on a day trip to the Festival of Britain. When we came back to Leicester we went to my grandmother's house. We often spent weekends with my grandmother so I knew that I would be sleeping in granny's bed. But on this occasion my mother warned me to slip into the bed without saying anything to grandma, who was already there sleeping because she had been very upset that day: her son, my uncle Charlie, had died. But Uncle Charlie was not an old man. He was about my mother's own age. He had had a heart attack. So death might strike even our family and even people in middle age.

I climbed into bed gingerly, trying not to disturb granny. But she heard me and turned her face towards me. She asked me if I had had a nice day in London and tried to smile. But her eyes were red with crying.

In the 1950s death was still a community event. When someone died the word was passed along the street from doorstep to doorstep and over backyard walls until everyone knew. All the curtains in the windows which gave on to the street were immediately drawn and would remain closed until after the funeral. In the summer this made the front rooms of the houses very stuffy and unpleasant. But the closing of curtains was the principal mark of respect shown towards the dead person and their family by their neighbours and friends. Then, on behalf of the Dorothy Road Fellowship, mother would organize the street collection to buy a wreath. I would accompany her as she made her way from house to house with a tin into which a suggested amount of money – usually a florin – would be placed and a record made. Sometimes we encountered people who had literally run out of money – because they were 'between jobs' or they had five children (a Polish Roman Catholic family) or because they were just poor managers. To save them embarrassment my mother would put money in the tin for them and mark them down as having contributed. Sometimes she was repaid. When we had done the round and made the collection the wreath would be bought and a note of condolence attached. Writing the note occupied a good deal of time: the words had to be right. Then on the morning of the funeral it would be taken to the bereaved family together with any money left over. My mother was always careful to ensure that there was money left over. Funerals were a considerable expense for older people and going into debt was something which decent working families could not countenance.

Death was still familiar. Until the National Health Service was created in 1948, people always died at home. The dying and the dead were part of everyday life. Even if the body were taken to the undertaker's, it was brought home again the day before the funeral and the open coffin left in the front room. Neighbours would come in and commiserate with the family and, if they felt able to do so, view the body. Etiquette required them to say how peaceful the dead looked. 'It's just as if he was asleep.' 'At least you know he died peaceful.' It was important that the final memory was a positive one. In this way the work of therapy – grieving and reintegrating – was borne by the community.

The following day the hearse would arrive and everyone in the street would come out of their houses and stand on the front door step to watch the procession pass along the road to the church or, more likely, cemetery chapel. This was not a matter of curiosity or nosiness but the way the street paid its respects. Old men who were not at work would take off their cloth caps as the coffin went by. Girls would stop playing hopscotch and stand still. No one left the street unacknowledged or unnoticed.

Working-class families set much store by a proper funeral. This was as much about quantity as quality: you were judged by the number of cars following the hearse – even if only one person sat in each! – and the number of wreaths your deceased spouse could command. I remember one or two spectacular floral tributes. A man died who was an amateur magician. Some of his fellow magicians sent a wreath in the shape of a top hat with a white rabbit leaping out. The widow of a man who had been something of a boxer in his younger days had a wreath made in the shape of a boxing ring with his favourite pair of red boxing gloves laid on top of it.

Sometimes the floral tributes were placed outside the house and neighbours would come and peer at them, taking their time in reading the attached cards and noting who had sent flowers and who had not. Occasionally a wreath would arrive from an unknown mourner and this would cause tongues to wag for weeks afterwards until the mystery was resolved. The street did not allow people secrets. At least, if you had secrets you were expected to keep them secret and not advertise the fact.

After the funeral the family returned for a ham tea, which my mother might be involved in preparing. This meant making a large number of ham sandwiches, some with mustard and some without, and ensuring that enough water was on the boil to keep teapots filled. Later on, when maiden aunts had gone to catch the last train or the last bus, the whisky would appear and serious drinking continue until all the bottles were exhausted.

The street also dictated patterns of mourning. Widows dressed in black or other dark colours for a year after their husbands died. Widowers were expected to wear black armbands or have a black diamond sewn on their gabardine mackintosh sleeve for the same period. Anything less than this was considered disrespectful and anything more was showing off. Remarriage was generally regarded with suspicion. My uncle Charlie's widow committed the ultimate sin of remarrying within a year of her husband's death. She was never forgiven.

Questions

1. Do you agree that the period 1960–80 was probably a watershed?
2. What were the main features of 'traditional death' in your community?
3. Is the collapse of traditional communities to be welcomed? What are the negative and positive results?
4. Is it possible to prepare for death in a hospital setting?

~4~

Death

The privatization of meaning

Man has created death.
W. B. Yeats

Death removes all meaning from life.
Jean-Paul Sartre

'I'm bounding toward my God and my reward', Cora sung.
William Faulkner, *As I Lay Dying*

Introduction

In the first chapter I suggested that as we looked back over the last century we could discern three distinct periods. The middle period, 1960–80, was a watershed, a time of transition, marking the collapse of the traditional community. As traditional communities disappeared so did traditional ways of interpreting death. Once again, Christianity was a casualty.

In this chapter I will outline something of the ways in which the understanding of death changed among the broad mass of the population and the reasons for this. I shall then seek to show how these changes impacted on the ministry of the church. Then, in so far as certain trends seem to have emerged in the period after the 1980s, I will suggest how the church through its lay and ordained members needs to respond in the future if it is to continue to minister effectively at the time of death.

The traditional community, pre-1960

When Parliament debated the 1944 Education Act which established the tripartite system of secondary education in England

and Wales after the war, some Members of Parliament questioned whether religious education should be made compulsory. This was not because there were objections to teaching religion in state schools, but rather because MPs could not see the point of making a legal requirement of something that every school would be doing anyway as part of children's essential education. No one doubted that schools would teach religion, and by religion the MPs meant Christianity; it would not have crossed their minds that any other faith (apart from Old Testament Judaism) would find its way onto the syllabus.

Until the watershed years of 1960–80 Christianity lay at the very centre of British identity. It permeated every aspect of national and local life. This is what began slowly to drain away from that time so that by the beginning of the new century cultural commentators and social historians could speak of the 'death' of Christian Britain.[1] It is instructive to compare a standard history of Victorian Britain with that of late twentieth-century Britain. It is inconceivable that the former could fail to mention religion; it is always a surprise when the latter does – even if it is only to mark its cultural marginalization.

In the first half of the last century, therefore, we find that the vast majority of funerals were religious and indeed Christian, mainly conducted by Anglican clergy using the Book of Common Prayer. What, then, was the Christian understanding of death as reflected in the Prayer Book? How did it shape the way people made sense of their experience of death?

Christianity taught people first of all to think about death: to face the reality and enormity of it; not to push it to one side; and to understand it as the end of the whole person – earth to earth, ashes to ashes, dust to dust.[2] Death was also deserved: it was the 'wages of sin'. If all this sounds somewhat forbidding we remember that Christianity proclaimed resurrection as well as death – Christ's resurrection, but also our resurrection. Death was real and deserved; but after death God would restore. The death of loved ones as well as one's own death had to be understood in that context.

Accordingly, the Prayer Book funeral service began with words from scripture that were both realistic about death yet also confident about life beyond the grave for believers: 'I am the resurrection and the life, saith the Lord: he that believeth in me, though he were dead, yet shall he live: and whosoever liveth and believeth in me shall never die.'[3] Entry into heaven, however, was by no means assured for everyone. The opening rubric of the burial service warned that 'the Office ensuing is not to be used for any that die unbaptized, or excommunicate, or have laid violent hands upon themselves'. Death might be the wages of sin for all, but there would be an additional payment for particular categories of sinner. Death initiated something as well as bringing something to an end. It had to be thought about very seriously indeed.

This understanding of death provided the broad framework in which most people before the 1960s thought about their own death, and the death of others and their loved ones. I recall as a boy being in a house on one occasion in the late 1950s when the doctor arrived to certify the death of the old man who lived there. The doctor was a gruff Scotsman, much loved in the area despite having no bedside manner. What surprised me was not his opening remark to the widow, 'So the old bugger's gone, has he?', but his attempt at offering sympathy, 'He'll be in a better place now.' I knew he was an unbeliever but he simply assumed she was not and that Christian belief in the afterlife would be her consolation.

The focus of the funeral service was the dead person and Christian teaching about death and resurrection. The words and rituals of the service were about the transition of the dead from this vale of tears to the joys of heaven. The only lesson set in the prayer book was from 1 Corinthians 15, in which St Paul speaks of the reality of death and the certainty of resurrection.

> Now is Christ risen from the dead, and become the first-fruits of them that slept. For since by man came death, by man came also the resurrection of the dead…

This, or something similar, would provide the parson with his text for a sermon. The preacher would speak about the Christian hope rather than eulogize the dead. The principal difference between the subject matter of the twentieth-century sermon and the nineteenth is probably the way in which the idea of hell was treated. During the course of the last century hell all but disappeared from sermons and addresses.

At the graveside the priest began by intoning, 'Man that is born of a woman hath but a short time to live, and is full of misery…' Then the final prayers were said which speak of the dead, now delivered from the burden of the flesh, passing to joy and felicity in the hereafter.

The mourners were not forgotten, though they were not the focus of the service and the comfort offered to them was not based on any psychological insight but on theology. The moment of burial – the thump as the coffin reached its last resting-place – was often a cathartic moment for them: it suggested absolute finality. Nothing was done to soften it. The mourners' comfort would come as a result of hearing the gospel of hope: their loved ones would 'not die eternally' and if they who were left lived the life of righteousness they too would abide in the sleep of death until the general resurrection in the last day. Then they would be reunited:

Here by the stroke of Love
Her love was rent.
Now are they one above
In deep content.[4]

There were other ways in which the traditional Christian message about death was reinforced. Every year since 1927 at the Football Association Cup Final the crowds sang the hymn 'Abide with me'.[5] This was the hymn which many, if not most people, would ask to be sung at family funeral services. It became the national anthem of mourners. It is probably the best statement we can have of the popular theology of the time. There is, first, the association of old age with death – which became the general experience of people as we moved from the time the hymn was written in the nineteenth century to the twentieth. Old age is 'eventide', the time of deepening darkness. The ephemeral nature of human life is keenly felt and poignantly expressed: 'Swift to its close ebbs out life's little day.' But death will not have the last word, the grave will not have the victory. The climax of the hymn speaks of the life hereafter:

Hold thou thy cross before my closing eyes;
Shine through the gloom and point me to the skies:

Heaven's morning breaks, and earth's vain shadows flee;
In life, in death, O Lord, abide with me.

Although there is no suggestion in this hymn of judgement following death or of the possibility that some souls may find their way to hell rather than heaven – which may in part account for its initial popularity – it is clear that in so far as people thought about death in the first half of the last century they did so using the principal doctrines of the Christian faith. The church was the authority in religious matters and the clergy were those who could interpret Christianity authoritatively. This may have been the last period of British history in which the church was able to exercise any major influence on the wider culture. When it all changed in the 1960s it did so with astonishing rapidity.[6]

The end of traditional communities, 1960–1980

By the 1960s the National Health Service and local authority welfare service departments were established and most people, as we have seen, spent their last days in institutional care.[7] This had a number of consequences.

First, it broke the links between the dying person and the local community, including the church. Even if local clergy had the inclination they no longer had the time to visit the dying regularly over a prolonged period when this was in a distant hospital. Neither did families or neighbours. Care of the dying passed to professionals – to doctors and nurses.

In the second place, care of the dead was also professionalized, passing into the hands of funeral directors and managers of crematoria. No longer under the control or even influence of the church, funerals and mourning became increasingly managed, perfunctory and utilitarian. The bereaved family put themselves into the hands of the funeral director, who negotiated with everyone else concerned including the clergy. Everything was now done for people rather than by them; even the giving of flowers was controlled – through the funeral director or the florist. Above all, time was controlled. Mourners need a certain amount of time to come to terms with the loss of loved ones, and the occasion of the funeral is important in that process. It is the time when those who grieve must 'let go'. It cannot be rushed.

Yet the typical crematorium service lasts little more than twenty minutes. Everything that is to be done and said has to be done and said within that slot. If there are readings and singing it leaves little time for a sermon to set everything in a Christian context and there is little time for the mourners to say farewells in anything other than the most abrupt manner as the curtain closes and the coffin disappears. (This contrasts markedly with a burial. Mourners can take as much time as they want throwing earth or flowers into the grave, looking at wreaths, embracing family and friends, returning to the grave over the ensuing days.)

The third consequence of the coming of the welfare state was a shift from burial to cremation as the municipalization of death – at least in urban areas – was more or less completed. (Anglicans had a near monopoly of burial grounds until 1850. After that date local authorities in the towns began to provide cemeteries.) Among other things, this marked the complete loss of control by the church over the length of time of the funeral, the architecture of the building and the type of liturgy that was possible. These were serious losses.

While there is a sense in which the form of disposal may not matter, some shift in sensibilities probably had to happen to make cremation acceptable. The total destruction of the body by fire, as opposed to burial, fits better with the idea that people are essentially spirits or souls and the body merely a temporary lodging; it fits less well with the idea that people are bodies and if they are to live again they will need to be resurrected in some bodily form, albeit a spiritual body. Cremation subtly undermined the doctrine of the resurrection and by the end of the last century 70 per cent of funerals were cremations.[8]

From the 1960s, therefore, new, more utilitarian patterns were being established. Death no longer happened in the community but elsewhere. Bodies were taken from hospitals or homes into funeral parlours by funeral directors and remained there until the funeral. Neither the family nor the wider community played any part in this process and as a result might never see the body. Cremation services at distant crematoria became brief affairs with ashes often subsequently scattered unwitnessed. Heavy mourning was discouraged, and instead of flowers, mourners were encouraged to donate to charities or organizations which had benefited the deceased in their final illness. Death was privately present but publicly absent.[9] We pretended that it did not happen.

But even more significant was the change in the way dying and death was understood in this period. The most obvious feature was that it was ceasing to be set in any religious context – until the funeral service. Professionals working within a state-funded National Health Service, even if they were Christians themselves, did not feel able to offer religious interpretations of death. The state and its institutions had to remain neutral; they could not privilege either religion in general or any particular religion. In any case, religion was increasingly regarded as a private matter. So death was understood in clinical terms and the care of the dying was interpreted to mean controlling pain and making people comfortable. It did not include helping them to prepare to die well in the religious sense of making their peace with God. The decline of the Christian vocabulary as public discourse for speaking about death dates from this period.

Three related developments can be discerned in this process which gathered momentum throughout the period and which continue – with some modifications – to influence the contemporary funeral.

First, as the Christian understanding of death began to lose its hold on the popular imagination and nothing very definite took its place, anxiety about how one would spend eternity gave way to anxiety about dying itself. This was not fear of the process of dying – though there will always be anxieties about becoming more dependent and fear of pain. The fear was the fear of ceasing to be – the fear of non-being.

For some people, anxiety about the loss of one's own existence can be made bearable by the thought that one's family continues. This reflects the Hebrew Bible's concern for children – 'happy is the man whose quiver is full of them'.[10] But in the 1960s and 1970s even this was threatened as the world seemed on occasions to edge towards nuclear holocaust.

This leads to the second point: because dying – ceasing to be – was feared, the death of someone became an embarrassment because it was a painful reminder of one's own mortality. This was exacerbated by the fact that communities had begun to lose their familiarity with death and were uncomfortable with it. People responded by shifting the emphasis of the funeral away from marking the death of the person to celebrating their life. The crematorium was often better suited to this than the church because in many crematoria the coffin was not placed in the centre of the chapel. The presence of the dead body could more easily be ignored – in a way that was impossible at a burial – and the focus shifted instead to the recollection of the person's life. In other words, the funeral service at the crematorium was turned into something like a memorial service; the body was present but it was ceasing to be central to the proceedings. This was a major change, which continued beyond the 1980s and became the norm by the end of the century. We might also note the way the funerals of some more public figures have been small, private affairs, while the major public event has been a memorial service.

In the third place, as the focus of the service began to shift away from the deceased as deceased and towards their past life, it also moved to the grieving family. Their feelings became of paramount importance and the service was crafted by the clergy, as far as possible, to make the situation more bearable for the mourners and to help them 'move on' to life without their loved one. The transition of the dead from this world to the next, and references to judgement, heaven and hell, ceased to be the main burden of sermons, indeed they might not feature at all; Anglican sermons in particular became little more than eulogies. Even the moment of final parting in the crematorium – the equivalent of the coffin being lowered into the earth – usually the closing of a curtain or the coffin descending from view – was in some instances avoided altogether: the coffin was left on the catafalque to be removed later after the mourners had gone. Many clergy came to believe that the main point of a funeral service had to do with the living not the dead – the immediate family rather than the wider community – and the influence of the newly developing counselling movement on this can hardly be exaggerated. This too was a major change and continued to influence those who created liturgies and those who conducted services into the new century.

In the final decades of the twentieth century, as people chose to live lives which were less and less under the domination of traditional communities, the traditional (which is to say, Christian) understanding of death began to be questioned more and more. At first people were simply uneasy with the Christian understanding and began to select and discard. But as the years passed they became increasingly open to other possibilities. Britain was becoming a plural culture and that included a plurality of religions and spiritualities.

We can discern two stages in this process, though they tend to overlap: selectivity and then experimentation. I will look at each in turn.

As the British ceased to be churchgoing they did not immediately cease to be Christian but they did become very selective in their approach to Christian doctrine: it was only part of the Christian repertoire that they were prepared to entertain. This was especially true in relation to the traditional Christian understanding of death. Unfortunately, our knowledge of the way the majority of people thought about death tends to be patchy and anecdotal; there has not been much research. My own understanding of what was happening came through reflecting on what people were committing themselves to in newspaper obituaries at this time. In 1989 I analysed the obituaries in one provincial evening newspaper over a period of one month, paying particular attention to those which were struggling to make sense of death. While most notices of death were principally factual – name, date of death, nature of illness, time of funeral – some went further as the mourners expressed hopes and emotions for their dead. This was sometimes done in (rather poor) verse form. That in itself was probably significant; here were sentiments which were better expressed in the more allusive style of poetry than in unambiguous prose. The mourners did not compose the verses; they were chosen by them from a menu at the newspaper office. However, since they were under no compulsion to choose what they did, we can assume that the beliefs and sentiments found there reflect to some extent the actual thoughts and feelings of those who chose them.[11] What conclusions did I draw from this brief survey? First, about one-third of all the obituaries used verses which were religious. The religion was not orthodox Christianity, though it was generally theistic and there were occasional references to Jesus. A shaky outline theology or understanding of death began to emerge.[12]

First, the verses assume that death is controlled by God. He determines whether and when we are to die; when he thinks the time is right, the dead are 'taken' or 'called' by him:

Softly through the shadows you heard God's gentle call
With farewells left unspoken you quietly left us all.[13]

(Many verses allude to the fact that the dead have departed without saying goodbye and this probably reflects the way most people now died in hospital away from family and friends.) The calling was often a matter of compassion towards those suffering as a result of illness or old age:

God saw you getting weary
He did what he thought best,
He gently took you by the hand
And laid you down to rest.

But sometimes it is difficult to ascribe a compassionate motive to what God has done; people are left perplexed by it:

He had the kindest nature
His heart was made of gold.
He was the finest man
This world could ever hold.
Why were you taken so soon?

When there has been 'much pain bravely borne' an unwillingness to accept death as deliverance can induce guilt which also needs to be expressed:

Forgive me Lord if I still weep,
For the husband I loved but could not keep.
Perhaps one day you will tell me why
You broke my heart and let him die.

However, although it may not be easy to part from loved ones, there is a recognition that having called the sick or elderly to him, God will now afford complete care and protection:

Oh, mum, it's hard to let you go
Because you know we loved you so,
But you were tired and in great pain
So God held your hand and took the strain.
We know He will take care of you
As we have always tried to do.

In general there is the belief that death is the gateway to a life free from pain in God's nearer presence and a confidence that the dead have passed to this new life. Sometimes this is called heaven. In this new life the recently departed will at once recognize those loved ones who have preceded them and will wait until those who are left behind join them:

A loving mother and my best friend
So kind and thoughtful to the end.
Look after her dad till we meet again.

If this seems to be the most widely held belief, there are some interesting variations. There is first the suggestion that the dead are 'sleeping' until that day in some indeterminate future when they will awaken to meet those loved ones whom they preceded (which is much closer to orthodox Christianity):

Each time I see your picture
You seem to smile and say
Don't cry, I'm only sleeping
We'll meet again some day.

Other verses make a different suggestion about our destiny after death. Some believe that the dead do not pass to another world but remain silent companions in this. In other words, what happens at death has an entirely 'this-world' rather than a supernatural reference:

Those we love don't go away
They walk beside us every day
Unseen, unheard, but always near,
Still loved, still missed, still very dear.

But the thoughts contained in the obituaries are not always logical or consistent. The family that had the above verse printed also expressed the view that their loved one was in heaven. Perhaps heaven is thought to be all around.

One strongly recurring theme in many obituaries is the idea that heaven is a place where God will correct the unfairnesses which are such a feature of life in this world:

> Put your arm around her, Lord,
> Treasure her with care,
> Make up for all she suffered
> And all that seemed unfair.[14]

Overall, what emerges is a form of residual Christianity, though it is a thin ration. There is belief in God who controls death. Death is terrible because it breaks family bonds. But it is the gateway to another life in which all unfairness is done away. Heaven is essentially a family reunion – like Christmas – and family members wait for one another in heaven and comfort one another while waiting. Those parts of traditional eschatology which are missing are not hard to see: there is no sense of judgement, there is no idea of punishment or the need for the purging of sin; there is no idea of the beatific vision: the sight of mam and dad, it seems, is reward enough. It is a narrow vision and hard to know with what degree of conviction it is held.

It is easy to mock what we find in these verses, but there are some important clues for pastors in all this about the British. In the first place, while popular theology of this kind is now somewhat removed from traditional Christianity, it does suggest that in choosing religious verses people were trying to keep the door of faith ajar. They indicate that even in a largely secularized culture, in the face of death, we are confronted with areas of mystery and uncertainty and want to assert that human life has a significance which is not dependent on the quality of any particular life – which is part of the religious understanding.

The emergence of post-traditional society, after 1980

When I examined the same provincial newspaper more recently, although poor quality verse continues to be a feature of obituaries, the religious references seem to be fewer. There are also new ones which suggest a rather different type of spirituality from that of traditional religion. We might call this new-age spirituality: people are experimenting with alternatives. There were three aspects to these.

First, people are understood as essentially spiritual beings for whom the important things in life are those which affect their inner or spiritual selves. At death, the spirit of each individual is united with that wider spirit which is the ground of all things in the universe.

> For Doug, now and always
> The wind beneath my wings.

Second, the influence of the green or environmental movement can be detected. Once thinking about death had been liberated from an exclusively Christian context, an increasing number of people began to think of death as the 'natural' end of life, and this too is expressed. In turn, some people began to look around for 'natural' means of dealing with the dead, and this suggested burial rather than cremation, and burial in more 'natural' settings such as woodlands and meadows, rather than cemeteries.

Third, in the face of the mystery of death, people still seem to want to say there must be more to it than oblivion. But what that more is remains a mystery and can only be spoken about in elusive and mysterious fashion:

> Only when you drink from the river of silence shall you indeed sing.
> And when you have reached the mountain top then shall you begin to climb.
> And when the earth shall claim your limbs then shall you truly dance.[15]

Taken at face value this makes little sense and would be easy to dismiss as simply sentimental. But again it suggests that the door to religious meaning has not quite been closed in modern culture. It hints at opportunity.

So far the religious verses in the newspaper do not seem to offer anything which corresponds to the beliefs of some of the other major faiths now numerically strong in many English towns and cities with sizeable ethnic minorities. But these beliefs are influencing the wider population. Anyone who visits to arrange funerals among the mainstream of the population will sooner or later encounter someone who says they believe in some form of reincarnation or some version of the Hindu notion of karma – that actions in one life have an effect in the next. For some people, karma has taken the place of the last judgement as a regulator of behaviour.

Summary

What are we to make of all this? What can we say with certainty about people's beliefs about death and its meaning?

First, we cannot even begin to guess what the actual beliefs of large numbers of people are. There is little empirical evidence and what there is tends to be of too general a nature. Pollsters have asked questions such as: 'Do you believe in life after death?' This means that pastors have little to guide them but must approach each pastoral encounter ready to pick up clues in the conversation; time and trust are factors here.

However, we can say in the second place that beliefs about death and its meaning are no longer securely anchored in or exclusively derived from the Christian tradition, though there may be a rather tenuous, residual theism. Beliefs are increasingly eclectic and fluid.

Third, people are no longer willing to accept beliefs because some authority – priest, church, sacred text – tells them they should. Beliefs will be tested against personal experience. If pastors are to speak about a Christian understanding of death their authority will not derive from their position as pastors or even from the hallowed tradition of the church; people will listen to see whether what the pastor says has been tested in the fire of personal experience and/or whether it resonates with the listener's experience.

Finally we should notice that what we find in the mainstream of the population is likely also to be present in congregations. We cannot take it for granted that members of the church know or accept Christian teaching or are not open to influence from ideas derived from elsewhere.[16] This suggests that teaching about the Christian understanding of death is either not being done well or not being done at all. My guess is that pastors assume that it is enough to say, 'We believe in life after death,' or 'We believe in resurrection.' These bald statements are not enough to satisfy modern minds that are only too well aware of alternative accounts of death which owe little or nothing to the Christian gospel. But, as with many areas of Christian faith, it is no longer enough simply to reassert old orthodoxies. A different style is needed in which issues are explored and knowledge and experience is pooled in the light of the Christian gospel. But the modern church strangely fights shy of teaching and learning; it would sooner be doing, which is why 'bereavement is fashionable, but resurrection is not'.[17]

Young death at the turn of the century

This is an account of the funeral of a young man at the beginning of the twenty-first century. The death of young people, for whatever reason, has become rarer as we move from the twentieth to the twenty-first century. The content of the service illustrates the diversity of views now present in the population and reflects the emergence of postmodern culture.

The young man lay in an open coffin in the sitting-room. He was dressed in what looked like a red football shirt and grey tracksuit. I gathered that he was a Manchester United supporter. He was good-looking, sun-tanned with dark hair. His parents and sister were there, talking, crying, sighing, smoking and drinking tea. Occasionally one of them would get up and go to the coffin and stroke the young man's face or comb his hair. He was 22 and had taken his own life following a disagreement with his girlfriend…

The family had been writing. Notes on pieces of paper were scattered in various places. They said that they had written an appreciation of him and hoped this could be read at the funeral. Was this all right? I assured them that we would be able to incorporate what they had done into the service. They also said they would like some of his favourite music played on tape. Could this be done? I assured them it could if they could let me have the tape. (I came to regret being quite so accommodating. In the following days quite a number of people wrote down their thoughts and wanted to deliver them at the service. The number of tracks to be played also grew as different friends suggested different pieces. In the end we had an hour of heavy metal – with sounds like 'a pile-driver screwing a score of metal dustbins' – to use a phrase of Peter Mullen.[18])

On the day of the funeral young people began to arrive more than an hour before the service. They came into the church and sat down, the boys with their heads in their hands, the girls quietly sobbing. Eventually there were almost one hundred young people between the ages of about sixteen and thirty. They did not speak. I told the organist not to play until shortly before the service. This was probably one of the very few occasions when these young people would sit for a protracted period in silence with only their own thoughts for company.

The service began: 'Jesus said, I am the resurrection and the life.' As the coffin came into view, carried on the shoulders of six friends, the sobs grew louder and one or two young women cried out.

I asked the congregation to sit down. I quite often begin these days by acknowledging that those present are likely to bring with them a range of understandings about death and what it means. While thinking their own thoughts, I ask the mourners to listen to what the Christian gospel has to say: God is the God of the living, not the dead; the dead rest with God until that day when all are called to account; in his nearer presence we shall know ourselves again and we shall know one another.

But I imagine that for most of those present the focus of the funeral is not the dead but the memory of the life of the dead. A memory, moreover, which is rapidly mythologized as a life without blemish. The truth of this was soon borne out on this occasion as we came to the tributes.

The young man's mother, sister, girlfriend, girlfriend's mother and other close friends came up to the microphone one by one and read from their carefully prepared pieces of paper. They recalled, often humorously, his exploits with cars, beer and women. They also spoke of his generosity and kindness to friends. This description of him jarred, of course, with the manner of his dying. Perhaps the pain of that was simply too great to acknowledge. So the emphasis had to be on a sanitized and sentimental view of his life. But this made his death into something inexplicable, for in all other respects this young man had everything to live for: a job, a car, money in his pocket, a family who adored him, a pretty girlfriend.

But what intrigued me most of all were the interpretations of death which his friends offered. These were often contradictory. One person said the dead young man was now with the angels in heaven; indeed, he was an angel. (More murmurs of assent.) Another said he had become a star in the heavens so that when you looked up into the night sky you would see him shining. Yet another said he was in the wind at your back, the rain on your face, and the flowers that turned towards you. One person said, in embarrassingly traditional terms, that he was with God; she hoped Jesus would take better care of him than we had done. (This was unfair for he had been indulged by his mother, doted on by his sister and adored by his girlfriend. Yet it produced nods of assent and collective sobs.) An older relative read a short piece which suggested that he would live on 'only in our memories'. Finally, someone read the inevitable words of Canon Henry Scott Holland to the effect that death was 'nothing at all' – surely the most absurd thing ever written about death by anyone, believer or unbeliever.

Two points occurred to me. The first was that anything can now be said about death and its meaning at a funeral and is acceptable, even if each offering contradicts the one before; each person is entitled to have their own opinion about death.

The second was more sobering for me as a priest. Several things that were said appeared to be statements of fact; but to treat them in that way would have rendered everything absurd. We knew perfectly well that this young man had not actually become a star in the sky or an angel or a flower; he could hardly have become all three. This sort of language was simply the means by which the mourners expressed their love for him; it was not to be taken literally. Was this, then, how the language of the New Testament and the liturgy was also being received?

Questions

1. How much of the traditional Christian understanding of death do you share?
2. Are there any aspects of the traditional understanding that you think are now unhelpful if expressed liturgically?
3. How far should the church allow the expression of other understandings of death in the service?

~5~

Bereavement

The end of mourning

Mourning is not the spontaneous expression of individual emotions.
Emile Durkheim

Introduction

The last century witnessed considerable changes in both grieving and mourning. The two are not the same. Grieving is our personal, emotional response to the death of our loved ones. Mourning is the behaviour which particular social groups deem appropriate in the face of death. There is a tendency for people to assume that grieving is a 'natural' and universal response, whereas mourning is determined by culture (or subcultures). In fact, both grieving and mourning are influenced by culture.

A striking and somewhat extreme example of the way grieving can be influenced by culture is found in the literature of the ancient world just before the time of Christ. A letter has survived from a man to his pregnant wife. He is working away from home in Alexandria and writes to her:

> Hilarion to Alis, greeting! Know that we are still even now in Alexandria. Do not fret if when the others return I stay here longer… Take care of our little child, and as soon as we have our wages I will send you something. When the new baby comes, if it is male, let it live; if it is female, throw it away. How can I forget you? So do not fret.[1]

Hilarion is clearly capable of considerable feeling: he loves his wife and child. But his emotional response to the death of a child is shaped by a culture which did not value every child that was born. Hilarion, it seems, can contemplate the death of a girl child without emotion.[2] (However, we don't know what Alis actually felt – or did. Perhaps, like Rachel in the Book of Jeremiah, she would not be comforted if anything happened to them.[3])

In Britain, a major cultural transformation took place during the nineteenth century and continued through the twentieth. This was a shift from death as community celebration to death as family event. Although the nuclear family can be traced back to at least the medieval period, Victorian Britain encouraged people to invest considerable amounts of emotional energy in their families and their spouses. Queen Victoria epitomized this in her marriage to Albert. Influenced by romanticism, people began to think of marriage as something you should embark on for love, not money or property – a view that would simply be taken for granted by the middle decades of the twentieth century. This meant that people tended to concentrate all their affections on a small circle of family members. When they died, those who survived were left distraught and the only way to cope was to demonstrate through elaborate and sometimes sentimental grief how strong the bonds of affection were. Again, we can see all of this in the reaction of Victoria to the death at 42 of Albert, her husband of 21 years. This is not to say that people did not grieve in previous societies, for they did. What was new in Victorian Britain was the almost obsessive celebration of grief.

The traditional community, pre-1960

In traditional communities grieving is public as much as it is private. There is a sense in which grieving is caught up in mourning. An important way in which individuals grieve is by surrendering themselves to the rituals of the community and the understanding of death implicit in them. In post-traditional societies grieving is done alone; but in the traditional community the whole community has a role and knowing that all your neighbours are with you in spirit is a source of strength for grieving people in those communities.

The Victorian age had decreed that mourning should be heavy, and that legacy lingered until the watershed years of 1960–80. Black was the colour of respect for the dead. Although much of the extravagance of Victorian mourning fell away during the Great War (1914–18), in the traditional communities of the 1950s it was still inconceivable that anyone would attend a funeral dressed in anything other than dark colours, preferably black. The whole community went into mourning and this helped the bereaved. One of the features of a death which many grieving people find disconcerting is the fact that normal life callously goes on. As a young man I remember being in a funeral car following the hearse with my mother's coffin and being (irrationally) very angry because the sun was shining and people were cheerfully going about their business as if nothing had happened: I wanted to stop all the clocks. In the traditional community, while normal life did indeed go on, for a while it was hidden behind drawn curtains and black ties. For as much as a year afterwards you could signal your bereavement to the community by your dress, and they behaved towards you in ways that were appropriate to grieving, suffering people.

We have already noted that until the second half of the last century the majority of people in England were buried according to the Book of Common Prayer. The assumption of the English Prayer Book is that what comforts the bereaved is the unambiguous proclamation of the gospel of Christ's resurrection. There is no attempt in the Prayer Book service to shield the bereaved from the reality of death in general or of this death in particular. Quite the opposite. The dead person is central to the proceedings, the priest 'meeting the Corpse at the entrance of the Church-yard'; and in sentences and psalms the priest reminds the congregation of the shortness of all lives and the fact that death is inescapable. The succour for the mourners which the priest cries out for as the coffin is lowered into the grave is not help for them to bear their loss but grace to overcome their sin. The comfort which the service offers is the knowledge that it will not be long before those who are left join those who are dead in a better place. The prayers are that this might happen more quickly. In the meantime, the mourners are 'not to be sorry, as men without hope, for them that sleep in (Christ)'. A stiff upper lip is the appropriate response for Christian men and women.

In this respect the Prayer Book stands in a long tradition in Christianity which frowns on too much overt grief. The origins of this probably lie less in the Bible than in a Christianity influenced by Greek thought (specifically Neoplatonism).

When we look at the Bible bereaved people are generally shown expressing considerable emotion in the face of death. Perhaps this is not altogether surprising since in the Old Testament, for the most part, nothing is known of any satisfactory life after death. Genesis tells us that human beings are only dust and their destiny is to return to dust.[4] The general view of the Psalter is:

> The dead do not praise the Lord,
> Nor those gone down into silence.[5]

Death is the ultimate disaster, cutting people off both from other human beings and from God as well.[6] It is not surprising, therefore, to find people greatly distressed in the face of it. Even the great king David has to retreat into his private rooms when he receives the news of the death of his son:

> And the king was deeply moved, and went up to the chamber over the gate, and wept; and as he went, he said, 'O my son Absalom, my son, my son Absalom! Would I had died instead of you, O Absalom, my son, my son!'[7]

Belief in life after death grows during the period between the completion of the Hebrew Bible (the Old Testament) and the writing of the New Testament. By the time of Jesus there is a lively debate within the Jewish community between the conservative Sadducees, who accepted the traditional view of the Hebrew Bible, and the innovative Pharisees, who taught the general resurrection of the dead at the last day. Jesus shared the Pharisaic point of view and spoke of the many rooms that were in his Father's house. Even so, Jesus is distressed when faced with the death of a friend: 'Jesus wept,' John tells us in the Bible's shortest verse.[8]

It was, of course, the resurrection of Jesus that gave the New Testament its distinctive teaching:

> For since we believe that Jesus died and rose again, even so, through Jesus, God will bring with him those who have fallen asleep.[9]

But what is the appropriate response to death for believing people? In the same passage as the one above, Paul tells the

Thessalonians not to grieve 'as others do who have no hope'. Presumably he says this because they are in anguish; they should 'comfort one another with these words'.[10] But it is when Christianity comes into contact with Greek culture that the idea grew that Christians should not grieve. Plato believed that people consisted of two parts, an immortal soul (the essence of a person) and a mortal body (the temporary lodging for the soul while it is on earth). Death cannot interrupt the life of the soul which both pre-exists its embodied state and lives on beyond the death of the body. Since the soul never dies, grief is misplaced. Neoplatonism, and with it the idea of the immortality of the soul (rather than the resurrection of the body), left a considerable impression on early Christian thinking. Among other things it bequeathed to Christianity what one commentator has called 'the triumph of immortality over grief'.[11] We can see this very clearly in the autobiographical writing of St Augustine – who was influenced by Neoplatonism. When his mother, Monica, died he closed her eyes and 'a great wave of sorrow surged into my heart'; he wanted to cry. But he believed this was inappropriate, for such emotions 'are the usual accompaniment of death when it is thought of as a state of misery or total extinction'. So, as a Christian, he held his tears in check; Christians, who believed in life beyond death, had to rise above these human emotions by an act of will.[12] (Why Augustine chose to be influenced by Neoplatonism rather than the example of Jesus weeping for Lazarus is another matter.) An echo of this, then, is the Prayer Book insistence that we are not to mourn as 'men without hope'.

In addition, the Reformers were anxious not to give any encouragement to the idea that the living could have any influence over the dead through saying prayers or celebrating masses. Consequently, the Book of Common Prayer funeral service has no prayers for the dead. The Puritans even argued for silent funerals.

In some contrast, the Victorians, prosperous and under the influence of romanticism, mourned in increasingly elaborate ways – though as people with hope. *The Times* pointed this out with dismay in 1875, and any number of contemporary novels contain descriptions of the funerary extravagance of the period.[13] By the beginning of the twentieth century even working-class families felt obliged to save considerable sums for their funerals. This was because mourning was a community affair. Large numbers of people were actively involved, carrying feather-pages, mutes, wands, batons and plumes. Horse-drawn carriages were draped in black crape and topped off with more plumes. When Queen Victoria died many people, including many working-class people, went out and bought black garments for themselves.

As the twentieth century progressed, however, two world wars and a long period of economic depression forced people to be more modest. The First World War in particular resulted in much simpler funerals. The war created a shortage in Britain of both horses and men; there was also a feeling that with so many men dying in such terrible circumstances at the front, elaborate funerals at home were out of place.[14] Horse-drawn hearses gradually disappeared – though they temporarily reappeared in the Second World War as a means of saving petrol. Cremations too encouraged more simple funerals. But until the collapse of the traditional community in the second half of the century, funerals with mourning rituals involving the whole community continued in both town and country.

Grief was ritualized in various ways: neighbours and friends visited the bereaved and viewed the body; in working-class areas curtains were drawn in the street; floral tributes were left at the house; men wore black ties and women black dresses; and after the funeral, close members of the family wore black armbands or had black diamonds sewn on their coat sleeves for a year after the death. Until the 1960s a funeral procession was still something which disrupted normal life and activity. People stopped in the street as the hearse passed; working men doffed their caps. No car or lorry would dream of overtaking a funeral procession, however slowly it was moving. That would be an act of considerable disrespect. Until the second half of the twentieth century the dead were buried and the continuing existence of the grave enabled them to be 'visited' and so integrated into the present. Above all, the whole community knew that you had been bereaved and it behaved towards you according to your new status – as a widow or widower or bereaved parent.

We should also remember that until about the 1960s, most people had very little time in which to grieve. Working men and women would not necessarily be allowed time off work, mothers and wives would have to get back to their domestic duties. We could say that work was therapy. There was no time to indulge in grieving. But after the watershed period people had more time to think about themselves and their feelings. They also had the necessary privacy. In the nineteenth century, the majority of people lived in cramped and crowded conditions. It was impossible to be alone for very long. But during the course of the twentieth century living conditions improved and increasing numbers of people found time and space to grieve privately.

One aspect of the religious context should not be overlooked, however: the influence of Protestantism. The Reformers rejected Roman Catholic teaching that the welfare of the dead could be affected by the prayers of the living. The fate of the dead was a matter for God alone. Consequently, they banned prayers and masses for the dead. The effect of this was to break ritual links between the living and the dead. One reason for the Victorian obsession with mementos and memorabilia of the dead was to establish such links.

Traditional communities, then, handled private grief in large measure by making it part of a community response and by acknowledging the changed status of the bereaved publicly. Grieving was done in the context of mourning. All this was to change and change rapidly from the end of the 1950s.

The end of traditional communities, 1960–1980

We have already noted that the collapse of the traditional community was accompanied by a more utilitarian approach to funerals and by embarrassment about death. The period of transition, 1960–80, was probably one of the most unsatisfactory periods in the history of funerals in Britain. It was also a bad time for mourners. Instead of burial, the typical funeral now became cremation. This had a double effect.

First, cremation meant that the time available for mourning at the funeral service was drastically reduced. The burial service began in church and was followed by a journey to the graveyard and a walk to the grave. There was time to weep and talk and reflect. At the interment, each mourner could pay last respects by sprinkling soil onto the coffin (a common custom in some parts of the country) or dropping a flower into the grave, or lingering over the wreaths afterwards. A burial is not rushed. But at the crematorium, everything was accomplished within half an hour. This was especially hard for married couples, who by the middle of the twentieth century were living longer, spending a longer period of time in retirement and enjoying longer marriages than at any other time in history. They now had to come to terms with the loss of their partner of fifty or sixty years in a service which might last little more than twenty minutes.

Then in the second place, cremation had the effect of making the dead disappear. Most cremations end with ashes being scattered, often unwitnessed. There is no lasting record of the dead, no grave to visit; it is as if they never were. C. S. Lewis says in an account of his own bereavement that he has a memory of a man who visited his mother's grave who said, 'I'm visiting mum.'[15] Lewis was at first appalled at this, but came to realize that this is one way in which we keep memory alive and keep a link with our dead. The existence of a grave also reminds us that the dead really are dead. It is a more realistic way of recalling the dead than, say, spiritualism.

At the same time, funerals – and so grieving and mourning – ceased to be community celebrations and became matters principally for family and friends; expressions of grief by anyone other than close family were discouraged. The pre-war and immediately post-war practice of whole streets going into mourning – by closing front-room curtains as a mark of respect until after the funeral or contributing towards street wreaths or standing on doorsteps while the hearse passed – gradually fell away. 'Heavy' mourning at the funeral itself was discontinued.

During this period it became commonplace to say that death had replaced sex as the great taboo. The utilitarian spirit allied to an increasing embarrassment about death resulted in the gradual abandonment of almost every other aspect of ritualized, community mourning. Flowers were frowned on; notices advising, 'Family flowers only', 'No flowers by request', 'Donations in lieu of flowers', began to appear in newspapers. Black gradually disappeared and, for a time, mourners were thoroughly confused about what was or was not appropriate dress. Grieving individuals withdrew into their families and were expected to be stoical.

Whatever they felt on the inside they should not show it. Where people continued to grieve in public or over a long period of time their behaviour was always in danger of being viewed as pathological. The death of a loved one was essentially something to be 'got over'. I recall visiting a woman a few days after the funeral of her husband in 1974. She sat in her kitchen looking disconsolate, barely able to say a word. Her daughter was with her and clearly embarrassed. When her mother began to sob she said, 'Stop crying, mam. You were doing so well. You don't want to let yourself down in front of the vicar, do you?'

One effect of restricting floral tributes to family members only was to make it increasingly difficult for people other than family to express grief. Families did not seem to realize that their loved ones might have had lives which touched others as well.

This was also the period when membership of the Christian churches began to plummet. Those who came to funerals from this time would be increasingly ignorant of the Christian faith.

So the period 1960–80 reversed the pattern of the traditional society in four crucial respects: the dead were made to disappear, grief was privatized, the bereaved were socially more isolated than ever before and the traditional (Christian) understanding of death began to lose its hold on people's minds without anything else particularly taking its place.

Perhaps it is not surprising that there was something of a reaction against some of the developments of the watershed period – though not all. As we have seen, most people continued to die in hospital, organized religion continued to lose ground and cremation remained the principal method of disposal of the dead. In addition, as people lived longer, with some spending their final years in states of confusion, some close relatives began to experience aspects of bereavement long before their loved ones died. 'Social death' and physical death began to move apart.

Then something new happened. From the mid-1970s a number of clinical psychologists began to write about death and bereavement, and from the 1980s their findings affected attitudes in the population more widely. Psychology now took over the role which religion had once occupied: it prescribed how we were to behave when confronted by the death of loved ones.

The psychologizing of grief encouraged the expression, rather than the 'repression', of emotion. For a while, psychologists and the gradually emerging and growing counselling movement seemed to suggest that there could not be real grieving without emotions being shown in an uninhibited way. The idea of what was 'normal grief' came to mean not what most people in fact did but what all people ought to do. 'Abnormal grief' was likewise not what was statistically unusual but what people ought not to do. Reticence and a stiff upper lip were no longer seen as admirable but the sign of a 'buttoned-up' personality, pathological. Such repression of grief could only have damaging psychological consequences.[16]

Psychologists began to describe the symptoms of grief, both physical – numbness, disorientation, the seeming unreality of the world – and emotional. For a while it was thought that there were 'stages of grief' through which everyone either did or ought to pass if they were to retain their mental health: anger, denial, guilt, acceptance, resolution. Therapists taught that the healthy person was the one who had 'worked through' the stages until they finally detached themselves from the dead – 'let go' – and achieved 'resolution'. They began to speak about 'grief work'.

Since Freud, what the various theories of grief had in common was an acceptance that the psychologically healthy end-point of the grief process should be the ability of the bereaved to detach themselves emotionally from their dead loved one. This ran against traditional culture in which the dead had not been let go of but integrated into people's ongoing life. This understanding was informing the work of almost all the professionals by the late 1970s. The clergy too were influenced, for by this time theological training had begun to include pastoral theology.

For a while it seemed as if talking had replaced ritual as the essential means of expressing grief. Therapy began to be offered to more and more people. A new group of professionals or quasi-professionals had become the experts to whom the man and woman in the street deferred.

The emergence of post-traditional society, after 1980

But the notion of 'letting go' began to be challenged towards the end of the century. By then there was a growing suspicion of 'experts' more generally. Michel Foucault had pointed out that we were living in an age of experts who sought to judge every aspect of our lives, telling us what was and was not 'normal'; people began to revolt against this.[17] Bereaved people in particular rejected the idea that they should break the emotional bonds between themselves and their dead loved ones – which is what resolution seemed to suggest. Those who trained as counsellors increasingly accepted the approach of Carl Rogers that they should be 'non-judgemental' and 'non-directive'. This meant that as far as the bereaved were concerned the counsellor should not seek to be prescriptive about what was and was not 'good grief'. Having said this, the idea of 'letting go' as the goal of grieving remains powerful. Professionals involved with the bereaved find it hard to give it up. An introductory leaflet from a hospice in the north of England, still circulating in the late 1990s, even though it acknowledges that grieving takes many forms, went on to say:

> An important aspect of bereavement counselling is to help people work towards making a healthy emotional withdrawal from the deceased person and to feel comfortable reinvesting their emotion elsewhere.[18]

But there was a major difference between the traditional era and the period after 1980. Previously, religion had spoken of the dead continuing in some other life. For the bereaved, maintaining the bonds of affection had this other-worldly dimension. Those brought up in the Roman or Anglo-Catholic traditions had no difficulty in praying for their dead or celebrating masses for them; Protestants found this more problematical. From the later decades of the Victorian period, spiritualism became fashionable for a while. But as the twentieth century came towards its close and grieving was allowable again, it was largely done without any religious framework; the idea of an afterlife played a less central role if it played any at all. In other words, by the beginning of the twenty-first century the focus was on the emotions felt by the bereaved; the dead, after all, were dead. The stages of grief were seen more as descriptions of possible states and frames of mind to be looked out for than as sequential stages which all must pass through on a road to resolution. But how was a secular society to allow the bereaved to relate to their dead loved ones?

Some people found the growing emphasis on the freedom and autonomy of the bereaved difficult. Traditional society told you how to grieve. Even the period of psychologizing had clear ideas about 'normal' and 'abnormal' grief. But in the new century the burden of deciding what is and is not appropriate falls on the bereaved themselves. Not everyone welcomed it.

In the last decades of the twentieth century new kinds of popular ritual began to appear. We first saw these developments at the time of the Hillsborough football disaster when a large number of supporters were crushed to death in the Sheffield Wednesday football stadium. In their bewilderment, and finding all the local churches closed (it was Saturday evening), distraught fans began to put scarves on the railings outside the grounds, light candles and leave flowers.[19] Since that time, small impromptu shrines have been similarly created at the site of fatal road and rail accidents and, most dramatically of all, outside Kensington Palace when Princess Diana was killed. In the past people would have laid flowers in churches or at officially designated memorials. This was a further example of people taking control – perhaps wresting control – in a situation that had previously been controlled by professionals. Paradoxically, it is also quite usual now for one group of professionals – therapists – to be suggested, or even demanded as a right, whenever a death is sudden or tragic or traumatic.

A further development has been the mushrooming of self-help groups, willing to call upon the expertise of professionals, but essentially finding help from the collective wisdom and experience of the group.[20] These groups are often formed by people who are all bereaved in similar circumstances – such as the parents of children killed in road accidents, or those bereaved as a result of murder.

Summary

The stoicism which bereaved people were expected to show during the period 1960–80 gave way to the therapeutic decades of the 1980s and 1990s in which the expression of emotion was encouraged. A 'stiff upper lip' was no longer admired but rather pitied: it was symptomatic of a 'buttoned-up' person who needed help to acknowledge repressed or buried feelings. Mercifully the tyranny of that kind of therapy is now largely a thing of the past, though it has left us with a general presumption in favour of showing emotion rather than being restrained. But there is a greater willingness on the part of professional counsellors as well as people in general to accept that different people will deal with grief in different ways. Some people deal with strong emotions by releasing them, others deal with them internally. And people have different levels of emotional response to crisis. What has been lost is the gathering up of more private grieving into community rituals; in the twentieth century we learnt to grieve on our own.

The end of the traditional community has also meant that mourning has become more problematical for people. There are few norms. People have to take their cue from what the bereaved next of kin signal, if, that is, they send any signal at all. One family will sanction more formal dress and be distressed if people arrive at the funeral without wearing black and carrying flowers. Another will resist any attempt to display more traditional signs of mourning and be deeply offended if money is 'wasted' on floral tributes. We can expect this to remain the pattern for the future, though we can also expect people to become more skilled at both giving appropriate signals and responding to them.

Grieving for a baby in 1972 and 1986

These two accounts are of the death of babies and the way young parents coped. The first happened in 1972 – the watershed period – and the second in 1986. In 1972 I was a curate in an East Midlands industrial city.

As I was leaving the vestry to begin evensong the churchwarden asked me if I had noticed a young couple on the front row. I glanced across. They sat together, staring ahead, seemingly unaware of everything that was happening around them. They remained like that throughout the service.

Afterwards I went to them and asked them what was wrong. 'We think our baby is dead,' the man said. I was puzzled. 'What do you mean?' 'When we got up this morning she wasn't breathing.' 'Where is your baby now?' 'She's in her cot.'

I took the couple home. The baby was indeed dead in the cot. It seemed that when they found her that morning they went into a profound state of shock. They had not yet sent for a doctor. They had done nothing all day until the evening when they came to church. Why church? Because it was open and because it was a place you could go into and sit…

Karen and Robert had been living together for three years in a small flat at the top of a large Edwardian terraced house. The baby was unplanned and although Karen had at first not wanted a baby, she had changed her mind during pregnancy. By the time the baby was born she was wanted and loved…

The funeral was unbearably sad. There were very few people present for they had almost no friends and Robert was estranged from his family who had disapproved of his partner. Karen carried the tiny white coffin into church and sat with it on her knee throughout the service. She appeared not to notice anything. They had requested a hymn, 'All things bright and beautiful'; but few felt like singing. At the end of the service she carried her baby out again and we made our way to the crematorium. The funeral director drew me aside. He was anxious now because Karen refused to surrender the coffin to him and still wanted to hold it. I said we would continue with the service. The final prayers were said and we came to the commendation and committal. I walked across to Karen and Robert and told them that when they were ready they should get up and place the coffin on the catafalque so we could conclude the service. They sat for several minutes – though it seemed like half an hour. The only sounds were the occasional sobs of the mourners. The funeral director began to look at his watch. The next funeral party would be arriving within a few minutes.

Then the couple got up, slowly, crossed to the catafalque, placed the coffin on it and stood there. I could not bring myself to say the words of committal in the service book in front of me; they were too violent, too harsh: 'We commit her body to be cremated, ashes to ashes, dust to dust…' I used the words of commendation only, 'Heavenly Father… we entrust this child to your merciful keeping…' The coffin trundled towards the small aperture. This seemed to jerk Karen out of her reverie and she screamed, 'No! Not my baby. No!' She tried to seize the coffin again but it was beyond her grasp. She sank to the floor and was inconsolable, crying out and pulling at her hair. 'My baby,' she called out over and over again, 'What am I going to do without my baby?' Eventually her husband and the funeral director helped her to her feet and out of the chapel. We were six minutes after our allotted time...

Some time after the funeral I visited Karen and Robert again. Karen said she could not get out of her mind what people had been saying to her. An older relative had said: 'One day, you will be able to put this behind you and have another baby.' Many had said: 'Time will heal.' It was all kindly meant, but for Karen it was received like a series of hammer blows. Each seemed to be saying that grieving was an inevitable process which gradually distanced you from those you loved until eventually they became little more than a faded memory. 'It was like my baby would die all over again,' she said. 'I don't want to forget. I don't want her to be lost.'

***

This second account is also of a death and funeral of a baby, this time in the late 1980s. Although quite traumatized at the time, this young couple did their grieving rather differently.

David and Jan telephoned. Would I help them arrange a funeral for their baby? They were not churchgoers but we knew each other through our membership of the local Labour Party. They explained that they were not Christians but they thought I might be able to help them plan the celebration (they refused to call it a funeral) for their baby and to say the final words over him. They did not want a service in church because they would feel inhibited in what they could say and do. I said I would do what I could.

The baby was their first and had died as he was being born late in the evening. It had been a great shock – to them and to the hospital staff present at the birth. They had coped in a remarkable way. When they were told that the baby had died they asked if he could be brought into the room with them. They then washed him, gave him a name, Adam, and dressed him in the clothes they had brought. The hospital had a Polaroid camera and they took photographs of him. Then, for the remainder of that night, they sat together and David and Jan wrote down their thoughts – capturing their sadness, their disappointed hopes and dreams, but also how moved they were by their baby's beauty. They told me that they would like to read some of these thoughts during the celebration and have pictures of Adam on each service sheet.

Over the next few days the young couple began to involve all their friends in their plans. Their closest friend – he had been David's best man – was a joiner. He offered to make a little coffin. When it came it was in oak with beautiful patterns and the baby's name carved on the lid. Another couple wrote a song and offered to play and sing it. A friend of Jan appeared one evening with a poem she had written. Others said they would provide a tea afterwards. In each case, doing something for their friends was both gift and therapy. On the night before the funeral we gathered round the open coffin which was placed on a low table in the centre of the sitting room. Each person present was asked by Jan to light a candle in turn, and, if they wanted to, to say a brief word.

The funeral itself was mainly secular. It was also sad, but not unbearably so – until David read their thoughts on the night the baby died. We heard of their shock and sorrow, of their disappointed hopes for the baby, especially as he was such a beautiful boy. People quietly wept.

My part was to act as master of ceremonies and to say the final words of committal. They were very clear that they wanted that. It had a finality to it, they said. So when everything else was done I stood to say 'ashes to ashes and dust to dust' and the tiny oak coffin was left for cremation.

I went away wondering whether what I had witnessed here was a pointer to the funeral of tomorrow: the bereaved will take greater control over it; they will celebrate the life lived, however short that might be, and not dwell on the fact of death; they will determine the content of the service and so the overriding meaning of it all. Was the pastoral role of the minister any more than enabling these things to happen – or was that dereliction of duty?

Questions

1. Is it easier to grieve if norms are laid down or if there are none?
2. What are the unspoken norms for mourning in your neighbourhood or among your family and friends? Are there any?
3. If you visit the bereaved would you find stoicism harder to deal with than emotion? Why is this?
4. Do you think we have to let go of our dead if we are to remain psychologically healthy?

PART THREE

IMPROVING PASTORAL MINISTRY TODAY

~6~

Dying well
Pastoral care of the dying

Dry your tears; for then all of us will be together, so happily, in heaven.
The dying child's advice in *The Child's Own Magazine*, 1856

No one really believes in his own death.
Sigmund Freud

A hard task dying when one loves life so much.
Simone de Beauvoir

Introduction

In this chapter I turn to the role of the minister with those who know they are going to die. Of course, we all know we are going to die. But there is a world of difference between knowing that at some remote and indeterminate date you will die and being told that your life is drawing towards its close. For most of our lives we live without giving much thought to our dying; we live as if we were immortal. But when you are of advanced years and feeling weary, or if you have been told that you have a disease which may very likely or almost certainly will end your life, the thought of death is never going to be far from your mind.

We must first acknowledge, however, that the decline of religion and the medicalization of death has drastically reduced the role the clergy have traditionally played with the dying even within faith communities. Roman Catholic priests report that they may not be asked to administer last rites as often as they once did, and a more secular community rarely asks a minister of religion to call on the dying to pray with them. This does sometimes happen and, of course, every minister is pastor to a community whose members also die. By and large, however, the minister today is involved with relatively small numbers of dying people and they are mainly members of his own congregation. But unlike the past, the minister may well find that other professionals now share his concerns. Among the medical and nursing professions there is a growing acceptance that in caring for the dying they have to have regard for the total well-being of the person – the approach is 'holistic' – and not just their physical symptoms. This is reflected in the stated aims of nurse training courses.[1] The English Nursing Board Course, for instance, boldly states that the object of training should be to produce a nurse who is competent in all aspects of care and who recognizes 'the total needs of the dying patient and the family'.[2] At one time it would have been assumed that the spiritual needs of the patient were synonymous with their 'religious' needs – and could be left in the hands of the chaplain or minister. But what British society discovered during the course of the twentieth century was that spiritual needs and religious needs were not necessarily the same, and while some people's spiritual needs were met by religion, other people's were not. 'Spiritual' came to be defined as 'questions about the meaning and purpose of life' with religion as one expression of that. It was also recognized that these questions of meaning 'surface with considerable intensity' in the face of death, 'especially in people who have not considered such questions before'. [3] This is not to say that the medical profession has as a matter of fact become more skilled in this area. The novelist Kevin Myers recently wrote this:

> Seeing my cousin pass through the last days of his life, as 11 years ago I saw my mother pass through the last days of hers, I was struck by how little the medical profession had achieved in dealing with the only certain problem it would encounter – coping with death. For all the admittedly great advances that have been made in pain management, the technology to superintend the departure of life from human flesh seems barely to have altered down the generations.[4]

By the end of the century, then, a distinction was being made between spirituality and religion, and those concerned with spiritual needs were a wider group than ministers of religion and included members of the medical profession involved in symptom control and palliative care. This was a new development in the twentieth century and it raises the question of the specific role of the minister.

There are two principal circumstances in which ministers encounter the dying person today: those dying in old age and those dying at a younger age as a result of a life-threatening illness such as one of the more aggressive cancers. Before we look at these two situations, let me briefly consider the pastoral qualities we look for in a pastor and the role of pastors in more general terms.

The pastoral role of ministers

What makes a good pastor? Is it a matter of learning specific skills or techniques? The contemporary church expends a good deal of time, energy and money in training clergy and others as if this were the case.[5] But being a good pastor is more like being a good teacher than a good car mechanic. A teacher can improve his teaching skills, but unless he already has certain qualities to bring to the classroom – such as the ability to enthuse children in learning and discovery – no amount of training can help. So with the pastor. What we look for in a pastor is the ability to relate easily to people, to make people feel at ease in their presence and a willingness to speak about personal matters. Pastors will have a good deal of practical sense, moral sensitivity and wide and varied experience. They will not easily be shocked or rush to judgement. But they will also be able to recognize the spiritual anxieties which lie within and behind the emotional turmoils through which people in deep distress are passing. All of these are qualities that would be shared with any member of a caring profession. In addition, the Christian pastor will be someone who can draw fluently on the resources of the Christian tradition and relate them to the experiences of day-to-day living. Being a good pastor is primarily about possessing these qualities. Questions of technique and matters of training can improve the skill of the pastor but they cannot turn someone who has no pastoral gifts into one.

The pastoral ministry of the church is in the first place a *representative* ministry. From time to time we hear the complaint that 'no one from the church' visited a sick or dying person. We then discover that several members of the congregation did indeed visit. What the one complaining meant is that no ordained person visited. Clergy may feel this is bad theology and reflects a less than adequate understanding of the nature of the church: lay people are just as much members of the church as ordained. But it does point to a crucial aspect of the pastoral ministry of those who are ordained, namely its representative nature. When a Christian friend visits the sick or dying, they do so as a friend who is also a member of the congregation. When the clergy visit they do so as the representative of the congregation. The visit of the minister is the visit of the whole church. When he calls he does so on behalf of all other members. The lay visitor says, 'I bring you my love'; the minister says, 'I am authorized to bring you the love of everyone at the church.' It is this representative aspect of ministry that underlies the work of ministers.

The minister stands for the congregation. He also 'stands for' God or the Christian faith. The whole point about ordaining people is that they should perform this role. When the minister calls, therefore, he is expected to be able to say, if the situation requires it, an appropriate *theological* word. This is because the Christian community has set him aside to wrestle with these matters and to be able to articulate something of the thinking and the faith of the church – which is that Christ has triumphed over death. This representative role applies to clergy. It increasingly applies to other accredited lay ministers, such as Anglican Readers or bereavement visitors, where they are becoming more and more involved in pastoral work.

If the minister has not worked through his own fears and intellectual difficulties he may find encounters with the dying deeply disturbing. Even where he has thought about dying and is able to stand with the dying parishioner calmly, there may still be moments when doubts and anxieties return. In the past we have assumed that clergy can only symbolize resurrection faith if they are themselves fully calm and confident in the face of death, but in the postmodern world people are not persuaded that anyone can know with such certainty all answers or have overcome all fears. In addition, this is an age which finds reassurance not in the absence of doubt and anxiety but in the acknowledgement and expression of vulnerability. One of the complaints that dying people have made of some encounters with counsellors is that they are too detached.[6] Ministers need have no fear of their own vulnerabilities being exposed; they may have to work hard at allowing it to happen.

What seems to have taken place in the post-traditional period is that even members of Christian churches no longer look upon the minister as the obvious source of authoritative teaching and incontrovertible wisdom even in the matter of death. The minister is rather a resource, or the means of accessing a resource – the resource of the Christian faith. But there are many resources available in the modern world and the test of this resource as with any other will not be its sacred origins but its usefulness. Does what the minister says make sense, illuminate the experience of dying, or does it fail to do so? The test of the pastor now is a severely utilitarian one. Except for a very small number of people within the church, the minister's credentials are not his licence to preach or his ordination but his capacity for wisdom and understanding, born of reflection on the Christian tradition, but reflection in the light of real experience. It is a taller order than it used to be!

With that understanding of the pastoral role of the minister, I turn to the two situations in which a minister tends to encounter the dying – death in advanced old age, and death from illnesses such as cancer in younger people.

Dying in advanced old age

The very old can often be quite matter-of-fact about their death. They can say with the philosopher David Hume, 'I see death approaching gradually, without any anxiety or regret.'[7] This can disconcert the less experienced pastor. In the circumstances of his active and enjoyable life, dying can only seem like loss. But older people have a different perspective. They know that they cannot reasonably expect to live much longer, but do not see death as cheating them of anything. They look back over a long and full life and are thankful for small and large mercies. They think with pleasure about the achievements of their children and their children's children. They have come to terms with disappointments and sought forgiveness for failures. They are interested in what is happening around them yet a little detached from it. They look upon death as the sleep of transition – from this world to the nearer presence of God, or simply to oblivion (the belief of some church members too). They may also find satisfaction in knowing that they will have a vicarious immortality, at least for a while, through their influence upon succeeding generations and by being called to mind in their church's annual remembrance. Towards the end they may also be very tired and find daily living an increasing burden. The thought of not waking again is a matter of relief and not a cause of anxiety – a view which may not be shared by all the members of the family or even all the doctors and nurses. Someone with this perspective can only find it irritating when well-meaning relatives or visitors try to make light of their situation by pretending that they are getting better, or will soon be back to a more active life. Ministers should resist attempts to make them collude in this. But what specifically do those dying in this situation want from a minister?

Although many elderly people approach death with relative serenity of mind, and do not necessarily want the minister to speak about the Christian hope other than in prayer, sometimes people do experience anxieties in the face of death and want the clergy to give some emotional and intellectual reassurance. The minister needs to be as clear as possible about the nature of the anxiety. One way of testing this is to ask, 'Is there something specific you would like to talk about?' Pastors need then to know what can be said credibly and how they can explain it in ways that carry conviction: they need to have contemplated their own dying and to have thought about it in the light of the faith. Those who are trying to come to terms with their death do not want glib and easy pieties about life beyond the grave, but some evidence that the minister has thought long and hard about the issue and faced at least some of the anxieties and questions himself. How he answers may be as telling as what he answers.

The visit of the minister may also be a reassurance that the one dying has not been forgotten by the wider community. Many old people spend their final days in institutional care at a distance from their old haunts and their old neighbours and friends. The minister comes as a representative of a wider group. His visit is saying, 'You are remembered – with affection.' It is easier to assure a dying person that they are loved by God if they are also sure that God's representatives on earth also remember them.

Dying can be protracted. There may be days when the person is fully conscious or days when they slip in and out of consciousness. There may be considerable swings in mood. On the whole, pain can be managed (though not always); there will be good days and bad days. But whether the pastor calls on a bad day or a good, his simple presence may be all that is required because the minister stands for the church and the Christian faith. Towards the end, all that may be asked of the minister is that he says some simple prayers, or anoints, or administers the sacrament. For those whose pain is being controlled by drugs – palliative care – their final days may be largely unconscious and neither the minister nor anyone else is able to do very much apart from watch and pray with those who may easily be overlooked in all of this – the carers.

Some ministers will unselfconsciously be able to touch or hold the hand of people they visit. This may also be reassuring for the person who is dying, though we should not assume that everyone likes or wants or needs physical contact of this kind. One person I visited in hospital said that she had thrown a vase of flowers at the chaplain because he had taken her hand uninvited! But it may be of comfort for people if the minister can leave a small holding cross or crucifix or prayer card.

Sometimes people who have been devout members of a congregation all their lives seem towards the end quite unconcerned about religion and make no request for the minister or his ministrations. Simone de Beauvoir noted in a memoir of her mother's death that although she had been a good Catholic all her life, as she was dying she refused all attempts to bring the priest to her bedside – which caused great distress to her pious friends. But she was simply too fatigued as a result of her battle with cancer to take part in religious ritual.[8] It may be enough for some members of a congregation to know that they are being prayed for.

Ministry with the terminally ill

The death of the elderly can often be accepted by them and their family as the welcome end of a long life. But when a younger person is told they have a condition that is terminal, death is not seen as the natural end-point of a life, but rather as premature and unwelcome. The line between an acceptable death and a premature death has been shifting for most of the last century as life expectancy changed. At the beginning of the twentieth century life expectancy at birth in Britain was 44 for males and 47 for females. If you lived into your 60s you were doing well. By the beginning of the present century, males could expect to live to be 75 and females 80.[9] Consequently, those who have to face death before they reach these sorts of ages are more likely to feel cheated. On the other hand, medical advances also mean that terminal illnesses are diagnosed earlier and people may have to live with that knowledge longer. What is the pastoral care that ministers offer at such a time?

Ministers will find it useful to have in mind what has been discovered about the psychology of dying. They should not assume that the dying will or must pass through certain 'stages', but it may help the minister to appreciate the state of mind of the dying person if these psychological states are understood: Shock, Unreality, Denial, Bargaining, Anger, Fear, Despair, Acceptance. They should not assume that each dying person will necessarily experience something akin to each of these states of mind; nor should they assume that they follow sequentially. But they are useful indicators of the range of possibilities and over time each pastor will build his own frame of reference based on direct pastoral experience. It is also worth bearing in mind that the relatives and close friends of the one dying may experience something similar, though not necessarily at the same time as their loved one.

Shock

When a person is told that they have an incurable and life-threatening illness it takes time for them to come to terms with the information they have been given. It probably takes longer than they realize. They may think they have absorbed the shock of it; but it is not until some days, weeks or even months before the meaning of what has been told them hits them with full force: they are going to die; they are going to cease to be. Then they may be gripped by fear and panic. Above all, the knowledge of their dying, once imparted, will never be far from their mind or that of their close family. They may also be unbearably sad when they think of the implications for others – their wife or husband, their mother and father, their children.[10] The pastor reassures that family members will be looked after and not forgotten.

Unreality

Those I have met over the years have often spoken first about a sense of unreality and emptiness that comes over them for a while after the news is broken. They go into shock. It is as if the mind initially induces a dream-like trance for protection as it gradually absorbs what has been said and all the implications of it. During this time it may seem odd or even shocking that the rest of the world goes on its way as if nothing had happened. One person said, 'I wanted to stop the car and shout "Don't you realize what they told me! I am going to die!"' The minister will want to reassure the person that the seriousness of their news has been understood and people are concerned for them.

Denial

Some people find it impossible to accept the reality of their diagnosis. They go into denial. They may say – to themselves if not to those around them – that this cannot be true. They may question the doctor's verdict. Was his examination too cursory? Could a mistake have been made, for one hears of mistakes being made? How competent is this doctor? They may demand a second opinion. Or a third. If they feel fit, they may clutch at that: 'How can I be diagnosed as seriously ill when I feel so well?' 'They are assuming the worst because they do not realize how fit I have been all my life. I can fight this.' Or they may simply refuse to talk about it. One person told me that when she was first diagnosed with an inoperable cancer she wanted to say to the doctor, 'Don't you realize who I am? People like me don't die.' It is not only the one who is ill who can go into denial. Families and friends may find it equally hard to accept the reality of the situation. Indeed, some dependent relatives or friends can remain in a state of denial far longer than the patient. 'We don't want to start getting morbid...' The unwary minister can easily be co-opted into strategies of denial by being asked to pray for a miracle of healing or by being asked not to discuss in any detail the medical prognosis.

Bargaining

Some people have told me that in their hearts or their secret prayers they have tried to bargain with God: 'If you cure me of this I will attend church more diligently and be a better father.' Even non-believers have been known to hedge their bets at this moment: 'If you do exist, let me get through this and I'll start to believe in you.' On the whole, bargaining seems to be one way in which a patient adapts to an unwelcome diagnosis gradually.

I have known members of my congregation to leave orthodox medicine at this point and begin the desperate search for alternative diagnoses and treatments. This can become quite obsessive and a great strain for everyone else. Pastors must pick their way carefully here. We need to offer support without colluding in deception. This is easier said than done, but it may be essential to do it not only for the sake of the terminally ill themselves, but also for loved ones who watch and wait anxiously. Of course, some alternative therapies may form a valuable part of palliative care.

Anger

The sense of unreality and the feeling of emptiness that those diagnosed as terminally ill at first often experience will in time give way to stronger feelings, both positive and negative. I have known people diagnosed with serious cancers who after the initial shock have reacted with what can only be described as euphoria. 'This is the biggest battle of my life and, by God, I'm going to win it,' was how one person explained their attitude to me. This may well be the first reaction of people who have a strong sense of personal worth and who do not feel particularly ill. But as it becomes clear that treatment is not going to lead to cure, as the treatment itself – chemotherapy, for example – leaves them progressively weaker and they realize that determination is not enough, relative cheerfulness may give way to considerable anger. 'Why? Why me? Why now? What have I done to merit this?' Or more sharply, 'Why is God letting this happen to me and my family? Why doesn't he answer my prayers?'

Patients can be angry with God, with the medical staff, with their family, their friends, even themselves. The anger is not unlike road rage – intense frustration at not being able to do anything that would make a difference to the situation. Like road rage it lashes out unpredictably and irrationally. If the minister is on the receiving end of harrowing questions he must deal with them seriously and gently make the best answer he can while recognizing that the questions really reflect the terrible pain of the person having to come to terms with an unpalatable truth.

Fear

When people say they are afraid of dying the minister should not jump to any conclusions about the nature of the fear. It may be fear about what happens after death; it may equally be anxiety about the process of dying. The minister should hear the cry of fear as an invitation to begin a dialogue and an exploration.

The dying person has many potential anxieties. He worries about becoming dependent and losing control over his body. He worries about the effects of medication, surgery, therapy. He worries about how he will cope in the later stages of the illness. He worries about how those around him will cope both while he is alive and afterwards. All these anxieties and concerns are real enough and have to be faced with a degree of honesty and courage. Doctors and nurses should be able to reassure about the progress of the illness itself and the palliative measures that can be offered. They can reassure about how the gradual deterioration of the body can be handled feasibly and with a degree of dignity. The minister's task is to help the person dying find peace of mind, concentrating on existential anxieties and what needs to be done to alleviate them. This may mean hearing a person's confession, either formally or informally; it may mean helping someone to see their life from a different perspective or helping them to see how they will still form part of the lives of their loved ones even after their death.

Despair

Almost all dying people experience at least some moments of despair, and this can add to the pain. Medical staff will explain to the patient that this is not unusual and the minister can reinforce what they say. The prospect of dying when one had so much to do and to live for is inherently depressing. Conversations often centre on the past and reinforce the sense that everything is past, there is no future. But in addition, some illnesses and some forms of treatment will leave patients physically run down and less able to pick themselves up psychologically. Those who have a strong faith and an optimistic personality may feel especially wretched at these moments – for they expected to be stronger. Christians who worry about their faith may be helped by thinking about the Lord in Gethsemane.

Acceptance

Gradually, most patients accept the medical verdict, diagnosis and prognosis. Everyone around the patient will now try to keep him cheerful since it is only too easy to give in to the disease and decline more rapidly. In the past, morale was often kept up by telling untruths about the seriousness of the condition itself. Now it may consist in telling the person that they are putting up a better battle than they are, or that they have longer to live than they could reasonably expect. This is understandable because the implications of accepting the prognosis are painful for everyone concerned. The dying person is not going to be here for Christmas, or for his daughter's graduation, or the birth of his first grandchild – or some other significant occasion. But often the families are protecting themselves as much as the patient. The minister should not collude in this but rather help the patient to use the remaining time in positive ways – setting affairs in order, healing rifts, making a memory box, receiving visits from friends and family.

One feature of the dying process is that as time passes the dying person withdraws more and more into an internal world – simply because it is no longer possible to get out of the house and meet people. They, and their illness, become the centre of their world. The minister will recognize this and the need for good conversations to continue about the wider world for as long as possible.

The needs of the dying

One writer has identified four basic needs that the terminally ill have and which we see reflected in the kinds of emotional responses they may exhibit.[11] Taken together, the meeting of these needs is what we mean by the spiritual care of the dying.

The four basic and interrelated needs are for self-worth, meaning, love and hope. The minister is concerned with each.

Self-worth

The sense we have of our own worth is the result of a number of factors, many of which are contingent. For example, we value ourselves because others value us. We are valued within our families as a husband or wife, a mother or father. The wider community values us for the work we do, whether paid or voluntary. But when we are told that we are dying each of these roles is threatened. The terminally ill person loses their job, gives up voluntary activities and may feel that they can no longer be a 'proper' husband or wife, father or mother. I have heard dying people describe their feelings as comparable to redundancy or retirement – a loss of usefulness – only many times worse. One woman said, 'It was like the day the children left home; I felt unwanted.' They also become increasingly dependent. It is hard to maintain your sense of worth if your greatest achievement in the day has been to walk unaided to the bathroom. It is hard to maintain your dignity if you have to be fed by another or lifted on and off the toilet. It is hard to believe you are still valued in a society which sets great store by looks and physical fitness if your hair has fallen out or your body has become emaciated.

There is also an existential dimension to the sense of worth. Death means that I am going to cease to be. Does this mean, then, that my life has never been worthwhile? Does death show it up for the empty, meaningless affair it always was? What does my life amount to if it comes to this? One person expressed it to me in this way, 'What is the point of *me* if next year or the year after no one will even remember I existed?'

There may also be a religious or ethical dimension. St Paul spoke of death as the wages of sin. Is my death because I am not a worthwhile person? Is it punishment – the just punishment of a fundamentally bad person in a moral universe? There are certain types of religious background – evangelical Protestant and traditional Catholic – which might more easily give rise to anxieties of this type.

The issues around the sense of self-worth are such that the dying person may not be able to broach them with members of his own family. They may not easily comprehend why these questions keep forming and the one dying does not in any case want to lay this extra burden on them. He may, therefore, value the chance to struggle with them in the company of a sympathetic outsider, the minister. This suggests that one of the more important aspects of this ministry may be the amount of time the minister can offer and specifically how much of that time can be spent alone with the person dying.

The minister may have to bear some of the dying person's anger. He needs to formulate replies, otherwise it will seem as if he is not taking the person seriously: 'You are not being singled out. It is nothing to do with your deserts. Cancer strikes randomly. God may not intervene. But you are valuable for you are a child of God. And what you have achieved in your life is of abiding significance.'

An important task of ministry is to reassure the one dying that they are indeed valuable and valued members of the congregation and the wider community. The fact that the minister calls is reassurance that the congregation values them even though they are no longer able to come to church. In prayer and the sacrament, links are made with the wider worshipping community. In conversation, the minister will recall past achievements. Above all, the minister will listen attentively to the person. In a variety of ways, the worth of the one dying is affirmed.

Meaning

When people are told that their illness is terminal their world collapses. Everything that previously gave meaning to life now seems reduced to ashes. The mental and emotional distress this causes (ideopathic pain) may also be accompanied by physical symptoms. One woman I visited over a period of about six months until she died could not at first talk about her approaching death without having panic attacks – laboured breathing and profuse sweating. Anger is often part of the initial reaction, but anger can only be maintained as long as there is point to it. Death even undermines anger as pointless. In any case, anger requires a lot of energy to sustain it, and energy is in short supply as the illness takes its course. Anger subsides in tears and gives way to despair.

Approaching death seems to mock the life and past achievements of the one dying. It threatens everything and seemingly the 'wise man dies just like the fool'.[12] The minister needs to give the dying person full attention and be sensitive to these existential anxieties. He may be the only person able to help. Although doctors and nurses now accept that healing has to be approached holistically, their principal focus has to be on relieving physical symptoms. They may have little time to deal with questions of meaning, or they may simply feel out of their depth. Members of the family and close friends may be too distressed to be able to deal with difficult questions. It may be too painful for them to be drawn into what they regard as morbid conversation, or they may lack any experience of talking about such matters. Relatives may even try to keep up their own spirits by not taking seriously any talk that suggests there will not be a full recovery. Sometimes a version of Christian faith can itself become the stumbling-block. If people have been taught to believe that God will always intervene when the welfare of his children is threatened, and only want of faith stands in the way, that can only create additional anxiety if the hoped-for miracle does not happen. We need to remind people that a miracle is only ever a case of remission: the sick that Christ healed became sick again; and Lazarus died.

The minister will gently probe how a person has made sense of life before and what therefore has changed for him. He will help him to see that his past life has an abiding value which death cannot destroy. The relationships he made in life, his achievements, the good times, were all worthwhile and valuable in themselves. In these ways he brought something of the love and goodness of God into the life of this world. The truth of that will be clearer when he comes into God's kingdom. Of course, there may also be unresolved issues that need talking through and perhaps some action taken – such as a decision to contact an estranged relative.

As the representative of the Christian faith, the minister already stands for the truth that meaning is not destroyed by death. He may not yet have fully faced his own mortality as a result of his own age or frailty, but, as a minister with pastoral care for the dying and the bereaved, he will have thought about the reality of death and its meaning in the light of Christian faith. It is assumed that he has confronted death and while he may still have anxieties, he has not been overwhelmed by them. His presence is reassuring.

Love

In life we are sustained by our loving relationships – with our family and friends and, for believers, with God. Death may threaten all or any of them.

Death clearly threatens the relationships we have with other people. It does so in the obvious sense that when it comes it will put an end to our time with our loved ones in this life. This may seem to undermine the value of all that has gone before, as we have noted. But doubts about those relationships can arise in any case. If the terminally ill are in remote hospitals it becomes difficult for friends and even family to keep in touch and that can raise anxieties for the dying person about where they now stand in other people's affections and concerns. Sometimes families can add to the problem by being over-protective, seeking to keep people away from loved ones because visits would leave them very tired. One woman told me that she had asked her husband's friends not to call during his last months because she wanted to shield *them* from the sight of him – he was little more than skin and bones – so that their last memories of him would be good ones. She would not be persuaded otherwise even though he approached his death wondering whether he had been forgotten. As he said, 'Have they written me off, then, padre?' But she said, 'I couldn't bear him to see their reaction to him.'

But sympathy for the dying also diminishes over time.[13] Carers can become hardened to the task – for their own protection – and others find the time needed for visiting becomes more and more difficult to spare as the weeks go by.

We have seen that the minister calls as the representative of the congregation and in that capacity brings the love of a group of people. His presence is a way of reassuring the dying that they are not forgotten and they are held in great affection. This is important to all that are dying but it may be of crucial significance to those who have no family or few friends.

The minister also stands for God. He assures the dying person that God loves him and his life is acceptable to God. Sometimes when people come towards the close of their lives they look back and regret aspects of the past. There are matters of which they are ashamed. They may have an image of God that is severe and judgemental and their minds might be filled with the unhelpful iconography of devils and burning fires. The minister needs to help the person to an understanding of God as loving, to hear informal or formal confessions, and give appropriate absolution.

Hope

We are sustained in life by hope – the hope that the future will be better than the present, or at least no worse. We are at our most positive when we have something to look forward to or a contribution to make. At first those with life-threatening illnesses and their families entertain the hope of recovery. They cling to every possibility – a new set of tests, a second opinion, another course of treatment, news of a wonder drug or new surgical procedure. Everyone knows how important it is to keep hope alive and to prevent the one who is ill falling into deep gloom. But when the hope of a cure or a miracle is dashed, for the person contemplating death any suggestion of hope seems empty. How can hope be sustained then?

Ministers need to help the dying and their families base their outlook on hopes of a different kind. Recovery is not possible. But dying well and preparing yourself and those around you is a realizable goal.

In the past, the concerns of the dying would have included if not centred around religious concerns: What do I need to do to ensure I go to heaven? Today, there is little concern with the afterlife. Those who believe in it, whether members of churches or not, take it for granted that they will pass into God's nearer presence and be reunited with loved ones. The focus of concern now is not so much on their fate in the life to come as their fate in the ongoing life of this world. Death, for instance, not only ends relationships, it also creates anxieties about how those relationships will fare subsequently. Those who approach death have questions like these in their minds: When I am dead, will I be forgotten? Will our relationship come to be seen in a different light? Will I cease to matter to those who love me now? Or, there may be a different set of questions: When I am dead, how will they cope? How can I help them sustain their love but without it being unbearably painful for them? These sorts of questions have largely replaced religious concerns about the life of the world to come.

Difficult though these questions are they do mean that the one who is dying is able to think beyond the point of their own death and to recognize that they can still have a role in the life of their loved ones. Can this be built on? One way of doing so is to encourage the person in the earlier stages of their illness to make a memory box (see Appendix 1). A memory box is a way of leaving something tangible for loved ones. The memory box is a small lockable box or tin into which objects can be placed which have particular significance for the person dying and their loved ones, together with letters, notes and photographs. Much of the contents of the box – though not the box itself – can remain a secret until after the funeral. The box is a comfort to the bereaved since it provides a concrete link with the one who has died. It is also good therapy for the terminally ill: it is something positive for them to do and they are comforted by the knowledge that it will help their loved ones after their death.

Planning the funeral may sound morbid, but again some people welcome the chance to do this. They want this last act to say something about them and how they made sense of their life and also to ensure that the service will help those they leave behind.

The emotional effects of ministry to the dying

I have occasionally heard pastors speak of ministry to the dying as a great privilege from which we learn a great deal. I am sure that is true. But it can also create in the minister a range of emotions that we need to recognize.

There is, first, the natural anxiety we share with everyone else as we are forced by the dying of another to confront or confront again the question of our own mortality. At the same time, although we are more detached from the patient than, say, the relatives, dying members of our congregation are our friends as well as our parishioners and we inevitably share some of the pain that the patient and the family feel. The minister treads a line between being upset and being over-emotional. But if he shows no emotion whatever, he may appear cold and insensitive, and that makes ministry impossible.

But we may experience some surprising emotions. If, for example, we have spent some time with the person, exploring their feelings in the light of the faith, we may find their subsequent mood swings irritating or worse. Again, if we feel unable to help the dying or their family overcome their anxieties, we may add guilt or a sense of inadequacy to our own small burden.

In the early days of ministry we are cautious about what we say to the dying, especially if we have witnessed anger or tears. We do not want to say anything that might cause more distress – a pressure which relatives may also exert – so our speech becomes guarded. Yet for the majority of dying people, what they most want is easy conversation where words are not being selected with obvious caution. If we speak about serious matters, moreover, it would be surprising if there were not sometimes an emotional response. We should not necessarily feel bad if the dying cry in our presence.

Conclusion

We can never be sure how any particular individual will react to the news that they have a short time to live. I have known people who were regular churchgoers turn their faces to the wall and go to their deaths in utter despair. I have equally known churchgoers draw on the resources of the faith, laid down over many years, both to support them in their last days and to inspire and comfort others. Sometimes it is the family that finds the situation harder to cope with than the one who is dying. The minister is someone who has unique access at such a time. He is an outsider yet also an insider. His role is to show concern and sympathy yet without being overwhelmed by emotion in the way that a close relative might be. This enables him to help both the dying and their family with the spiritual task of making sense of what is happening by setting it all in the context of the Christian hope.

Pastors can help families face hard truths if they know a family well or can build a good rapport with them quickly. Unlike other members of the congregation, the minister's visit is rarely questioned; he is expected to call; he is generally always welcome and admitted to a house. Much of the pastoral task consists in helping all concerned to deal with the situation of approaching death by offering the kind of human help which anyone can give. But the minister also stands for a Christian congregation and for God. It is always appropriate for him to speak about matters of faith and to pray. Indeed, it is expected of him.

Dying in old age

My father died in 1998 at the age of 84. He had been ill for some time and died in a nursing home. In this respect his death is a typically modern death. It is easy to criticize nursing home care, or to feel guilty about putting our loved ones into homes, but perhaps there is more to be said.

When my father was diagnosed as having cancer of the lung, the doctor did not call it 'cancer' but spoke rather of 'a patch on the lungs', the result of smoking twenty cigarettes a day all his life. Whether my father misunderstood or simply chose to ignore what the doctor said, none of us ever knew. For he belonged to the old school who had fought in the world war and regarded any discussion by men of such intimate matters as your own ill-health as unforgivable weakness. He just would not talk about 'unpleasantness' even if the unpleasantness was his own terminal illness. Push disagreeable things to one side, control your feelings, give nothing away, we can get through –these were the watchwords that had guided my father's conduct all through his life. He was not going to be any different in the face of death.

By this time he was in a nursing home near to my brother, but 140 miles from me. He had finally become quite unable to take care of himself in his own home and could no longer be left by himself. Since my brother and I worked we felt we had little alternative other than to find a nursing home. In order to finance this we took powers of attorney to sell his house – though we never told him and he never asked. He had always said, 'I haven't any money to leave but at least you'll have the house.'

Should we try to get him to face the truth? Was his inability to 'hear' what the doctor said 'denial'? Or was it his way of coping? If it was his way of coping, who were we to tell him to handle the situation differently? He was not going to learn new mechanisms for dealing with life now. It made it hard for us because we wanted to talk openly about his dying and do all the things you are supposed to do at such a time. We wanted to remind him of all the good things he had done and his achievements. We wanted to fill the gaps in our own knowledge about the family. We wanted to bring our children to receive some final last benediction. We wanted to talk about the sort of service he would like and to assure him that afterwards his mortal remains would be laid to rest near to Dorothy, his wife and our mother. But he would not allow any of this to happen. If the conversation seemed to be straying too far in the direction of personal matters he would sigh, say he was tired, and turn away. At first I thought he did not realize the gravity of his illness and its outcome. I came to think that he knew only too well the implications of what the doctor had said to him, but to say it aloud would change everything. We would stop having cheerful, chatty conversations about this and that and start behaving like people who are visiting the dying. This, I now believe, is what he wanted at all costs to avoid. He wanted to enjoy what he could of each day without being burdened by the thought that he ought to put his affairs in order – he was too tired for that. I realized how tired he was when he signed without protest the power of attorney form (so that we could sell his house to pay for his care). He wanted us, when we visited, to be light-hearted, to chat, to joke, so that when we left he would have pleasant memories and funny stories to call to mind. So he refused to face the truth about his illness openly, not because he feared death but because he feared what we would do to the quality of the moments he had left if we visited a dying man rather than a frail old man in a nursing home.

But what about the consolations of religion? He had been brought up an Anglo-Catholic and knew about the role of the priest at the time of death. He could have asked for the sacrament or to make his confession. He did neither. He was non-committal when I asked him if he would like the parish priest to call – so I did not press the point. Nor did he ever say anything directly about the form of funeral service he would like. I think the reason for this is that if he had asked for anything it would have been a tacit acknowledgement that he was dying and again it would have affected the way we dealt with him in these last days. But he had his beliefs and they sustained him. And he knew his church would sing a joyful funeral – which they did. In this respect my father caused us to behave towards him very much as Judaism has traditionally schooled people to behave towards the dying – by doing nothing to break a person's morale. There is no tradition of preparing for death in Judaism, only of hoping to the end.[14] Perhaps there is wisdom in this.

He had always been a very independent person – to the point of stubbornness. Yet in the end he went to the nursing home without protest. I think he was by then very weary. He had nursed my mother during her last illness, and he had been very lonely after she died. He had seen his two sons marry and have families of their own. He had enjoyed his last job as a technician at the university and his membership of the local church. Now he was quite ready to go. I thought he would hate having people fuss over him in the home, but the reverse seems to have been the case. He relished being looked after, having meals provided, not having to do the shopping or the cooking or the washing up, or, above all, having to think about it. He enjoyed chatting with the staff and teasing them, especially the younger women. They treated him as if he were their dad; he looked upon them as his daughters. The daughters he had always wanted and never had. I am not sure whether the quality of his life towards the end could have been improved either by staying in his own home or by living with either my brother or myself.

Questions

1. What do you think a 'good death' would be?
2. Does it matter if a person is in denial about the gravity of their illness?
3. How far can a Christian pastor minister to a non-believer who is dying?
4. If resources are limited and the population is ageing, would a more sensible policy option be to support an expansion of nursing homes rather than enabling people to stay in their own homes?

~7~

Taking a funeral

Handling emotions and setting in perspective

The funeral, therefore, is for those who are left.
Wesley Carr, *Brief Encounters*

My mother comes in to say that she has rung the vicar – it is not yet eight, so he can say a prayer at matins and word will get round the village without our having to phone: the church still has its uses after all.
Blake Morrison, *And When Did You Last See Your Father?*

Introduction

Representatives of the Christian churches continue to conduct the overwhelming majority of funerals held in Britain. It is an important ministry. Unlike weddings, there are as yet few alternatives to a funeral taken by the local minister. If, however, Christian ministers are to retain the trust of the majority in this increasingly plural culture we need to be much more thoughtful about what we are doing and work continuously to improve what we offer. In particular, we need to bear in mind – as we noted in Chapter 3 – that people in the future may want to play a greater role in preparing for their own deaths and planning their funerals.

Every funeral divides into three moments: the pre-funeral visit, the funeral service and the follow-up. In this chapter I will consider each in turn and ask in each case, What is it for?

The pre-funeral visit

The purpose of the pre-funeral visit is fourfold:

to agree the essential details of the funeral service and ensure that the wishes of the bereaved are articulated and then carried through;
to gather all necessary information about the deceased;
to make some assessment about the pastoral needs of the bereaved;
to reassure the bereaved that the funeral of their loved one will be taken competently and well.

When the funeral director telephones to say that a death has occurred the minister contacts the next of kin at once and seeks to visit immediately. There are a number of reasons for this sense of urgency: the bereaved will be busy in the next few days, or may go to stay with a relative and be hard to find; the minister needs to establish some rapport with people he may never have met before; there may be particular requests for readings or music which will require some research. Above all, we know that people die in many different ways and circumstances and until we visit we cannot be sure what the significance of this death is to those who mourn. The bereaved will feel most helped by a funeral if they feel that its construction has been a partnership between themselves and the minister.

Some ministers are hostile to funeral directors. This is often unfair and certainly counterproductive. Ministers have to bear in mind that they have generally been drawn into matters at a relatively late stage. The funeral director has already been involved with the family, the hospital, possibly the coroner, the crematorium or graveyard authority. In most places, though especially in busy urban areas, they are under considerable pressure as they seek to make all the necessary arrangements in a relatively short period of time and meet the requests of the bereaved as to the timing of the funeral. As far as possible, ministers should seek to fit in with the funeral director's timetable – which is largely dictated by others – rather than impose their own. A minister's pastoral ministry is made less effective if they give a funeral director the impression that they are awkward to deal with. Nor should ministers underestimate the pastoral role that many funeral directors undoubtedly play. They are usually in contact with the bereaved before the minister and may already have been pastorally helpful to them. As a profession they generally pride themselves on their pastoral manner; they also know that if they do not develop good pastoral skills they may find themselves losing business. Most families will be very grateful for the role they perform and only too pleased to be able to put themselves into the hands of a competent professional at such a time.

This is not to say that funeral directors always get things right. The basic information which funeral directors supply to a minister about the deceased can sometimes be (unintentionally) misleading. We are informed that George Jones has died aged 72 and the next of kin is his widow, Mrs Doreen Jones, at the same address. However, when we visit and talk to the bereaved we discover that George was always known as Bill and although he had always lived with his wife Doreen, the person he had been closest to was actually Dolly, his mistress of fifteen years and the mother of two of his children.

As we engage the bereaved in gentle conversation the story of their loved one's life gradually emerges and pastors quickly learn not to be surprised or shocked by anything they are told. If we are to say something by way of a tribute we need to make careful judgements about how much we say and how much we leave unsaid. One useful technique is to write down the phrases the mourners themselves use about the deceased and then repeat them in the tribute – though we bear in mind that some phrases may not be appropriate in a more public setting. The purpose of a tribute, however, is not to say everything that might be said but to point to significant moments in the life of the deceased or significant aspects of their character which will enable all those present at the funeral to think their own individual thoughts. We offer triggers for the recollection of more intimate and personal memories. It is worth remembering that no one will know the deceased in every aspect of his or her life so it may be important to supplement the information the family give by talking to friends and neighbours. We not only tell each mourner something which he or she already knows, we also introduce them to a more rounded account of the one who has died – which is why we need to touch on a person's working life, their hobbies and interests, as well as their family life. Part of the minister's task in any case is to help the bereaved realize that the funeral is a community event as much as a family occasion. There will be others present who also knew the deceased and they will want their part in his or her life acknowledged and their chance to grieve at his or her passing.[1]

Occasionally we are told about some dark part of the deceased's past or present, or we gather they were thoroughly unpleasant in some way. It may be appropriate to allude to this without spelling out matters in any detail. There will be some occasions where not doing so would be unhelpful to those who mourn. We should certainly never seek to idealize anyone's life. Fortunately, modern liturgies will acknowledge in a general way the need for the healing of the 'memories of hurt and failure' and there is no need to repeat this in the address. We should not underestimate the importance of the liturgy in acknowledging and dealing with difficulties of this kind.

We should never make assumptions about a death simply on the basis of the bare information supplied to us by the funeral director. George Jones died in hospital after a stroke. This is what appears on the death certificate. But Doreen believes the stroke was triggered by the shock of having one of his children predecease him the previous year. While not necessarily accepting any causal link between the two, it might be helpful to Doreen to acknowledge that this is what she felt.

If the churches are to retain the confidence of people in the future, ministers will have to be sensitive to the type of service mourners want and to the sort of sentiments they want expressed. We live in a consumer culture where people are used to saying what they want and expressing dissatisfaction if they do not get it. This is not to suggest that mourners should wholly dictate the form of the service, for which, in any case, in denominations with a strong liturgical tradition there will be limited scope. But each funeral is the result of a unique partnership between minister and bereaved, the product of negotiation not dictation. There is an important sense in which the minister is doing what the bereaved would like to do themselves but know that in their fragile state they cannot. It is important, therefore, for the minister to gauge accurately what this family would like to hear said and have done. It is entirely possible to keep the Christian liturgical framework and still include elements or emphasize themes that mean a lot to the bereaved but are not at the forefront of the liturgy. Even if we are told that the deceased was not a believer, the minister can acknowledge this and retain integrity for what is done. I recently said this at the beginning of a service for a man who was well known in a local pub for his scathing comments about the church: 'Although, as you may know, Jack was not a believer, Jill is, and she very much wanted a Christian service for her husband. This is her way as a Christian of saying her goodbye to him. It will help Jill; and because she believes Christianity is true, she does not doubt that it will help Jack as well.' It would have been very difficult for everyone to participate with any integrity if we had not acknowledged Jack's position and given some justification for what we were doing. I also included prayers that referred to 'those whose faith is known to you alone'. In a highly plural society situations of this kind will occur more frequently.

The pre-funeral visit enables ministers to make some assessment of the pastoral needs of the bereaved – for each bereaved person is different and one can never presume how people are going to react. The minister may relate what he discovers to some broad theory about the stages of grief – anger, denial, guilt, acceptance, resolution. However, he should recognize that the assessment is inevitably inadequate given the brevity of the contact, and it occurs in any case in the very early days of bereavement. If grieving is a process which can take anything from two to five years, what the minister finds on a pre-funeral visit is a person who is only at the start of a journey. Perhaps a better guide is to seek the answer to a few simple practical questions: Is the bereaved person alone? How well do they seem to be coping? Have they seen their doctor? Would they welcome a visit from a parish (bereavement) visitor?

Bereaved people are not always able to take in or remember what has been said in these conversations. The wise pastor will leave behind some record of what has been agreed and how the minister can be contacted should the need arise.[2]

Finally, the pre-funeral visit is a key element in assuring the bereaved person that the funeral of their loved one will be conducted competently and well. The bereaved person may not take in everything that is said; but they will form an impression of the minister as someone who is sympathetic, interested, concerned, listening, thoughtful, competent – or not. This goes to the heart of pastoral ministry. What the bereaved look for in the minister – albeit at a less than conscious level – are both personal qualities and professional. They want a person who can quickly and easily engage with them as a fellow human being – someone who has also known sorrow, or who is willing to make the imaginative effort to understand something of what they are going through. Yet equally they want a professional pastor who will understand and deal with emotion without being overwhelmed by it and will competently do whatever has to be done to conduct the funeral well. As a religious professional the minister is also expected to stand for faith in the face of death. He or she may have had their own struggles and uncertainties; but they have come through. They can give an account of how it is possible to believe in the love of God in circumstances which seem to contradict it. One way in which this religious competence can be established is to pray with the bereaved.

The bereaved need to know that the funeral will be done well because, confused though they are, they know that what happens is important. It will be one of the key events in their life with the deceased. They will think about it many times in the years to come.

The funeral service

According to the Dutch anthropologist Arnold van Gennep, if human beings are to survive the traumatic change which the death of a loved one brings, they need rituals which will help them deal with their loss not only intellectually but even more crucially at the level of feeling. Specifically, the bereaved need to adopt a new perspective, to recognize that the future is going to be a future without the deceased, and to make the transition to that different future. One important purpose of the funeral for them is to say that this transition is possible – though it may take time.

Van Gennep identifies three types of ritual as necessary to achieve this transition which he calls pre-liminal, liminal and post-liminal rites.[3] The pre-liminal rite enables the bereaved to acknowledge the reality of death and to separate from the dead loved one. The liminal rite involves the transition which the bereaved must make if they are to live without their loved one.

The post-liminal rite is concerned with the reincorporation of the bereaved into society, though living now without their loved one. In some cultures the enactment of each of these rites might take some considerable time. In modern British culture the ritual acknowledgement of death is often compressed into little more than the funeral service itself. This is not to say that everything can be accomplished during the course of a 20-minute service at a crematorium. The sort of changes that bereaved people have to make take time – often more time than anyone could imagine. But the funeral service can signal the shape of the changes that have to be made, and the cost of those changes, even if working them through will only happen over a much longer period of time. If we examine modern funeral liturgies (I will concentrate on the funeral liturgy of the Anglican Church as we have it in *Common Worship*), we can see these three moments – pre-liminal, liminal and post-liminal – acknowledged.

Acknowledging the reality of death

The funeral service usually takes place in the early days of a person's bereavement. As such it serves to bring what has happened into focus. In the first place this means understanding the funeral as a *rite de passage* for the dead; and because of that it speaks unambiguously of the reality of death to the living. It helps the bereaved to acknowledge the death of their loved one and to begin to make the separation from them as still alive. Sometimes mourners may have viewed the body in a chapel of rest beforehand. Sometimes they may have received the body at home before the funeral. But these practices are not as common as they once were. For many people, if not most people, there will have been no contact with the dead from the time of the death – and possibly not even then – until the day of the funeral. *Common Worship* provides for the reception of the body before the service when the minister may, for example, sprinkle the coffin with water and family and friends may cover it with a pall and place a Bible or cross on it. Symbols of the life and faith of the deceased may also be placed on or near it. But if these are not already the traditions of a church or a family it is unlikely that there will be much use of this provision. For the majority of mourners, the only funeral rite they will attend will be the funeral service itself.

If the funeral service is in a church, the coffin is placed in a very central position – perhaps with the Paschal (Easter) candle beside it. This is not always so in a crematorium where catafalques are often far from central and are sometimes so arranged that the coffin is scarcely visible to most of the congregation. However, this is the moment where the human community acknowledges the bleak reality of death, marking the separation of the deceased from the living and the transition of the dead from this world to whatever comes after. In older liturgies, such as the Book of Common Prayer, this was almost the only focus of the rite. In modern forms of service, while many other notes are sounded as well, this aspect is emphasized at particular moments and gives general shape to the service as a whole. So, for example, in *Common Worship*, the minister begins by stating that the service serves a number of purposes including the marking of the transition of the dead:

> We have come here today
> to remember before God our brother/sister N;
> to give thanks for his/her life;
> to commend him/her to God our merciful redeemer and judge;
> to commit his/her body to be buried/cremated,
> and to comfort one another in our grief.

More specifically, of course, there is the moment of commendation:

> We entrust N to your mercy…

The note of transition is even more pronounced in the funeral of children. These are the words for an older child:

> To you, gentle Father,
> we humbly entrust this child so precious in your sight.
> Take him/her into your arms
> and welcome him/her into your presence
> where there is no sorrow nor pain,
> but the fullness of peace and joy with you
> for ever and ever.

Again, in one of the alternative prayers of commendation (which may also be used with the dying), the theme of transition is unmistakable:

> N, go forth from this world:
> in the love of God the Father who created you,
> in the mercy of Jesus Christ who redeemed you,
> in the power of the Holy Spirit who strengthens you.
> May the heavenly host sustain you
> and the company of heaven enfold you.
> In communion with all the faithful,
> may you dwell this day in peace.[4]

And at the committal of the body to the ground or to cremation the idea of transition is again at the forefront:

> We have entrusted our brother/sister N to God's mercy, and
> we now commit his/her body to the ground:
> earth to earth, ashes to ashes, dust to dust;
> In sure and certain hope of the resurrection to eternal life
> through our Lord Jesus Christ,
> who will transform our frail bodies
> that they may be conformed to his glorious body…

Marking this transition ritually helps the bereaved to say farewell and acknowledge that the person we knew is one whom we 'see no more'; they are no longer present to us, but begin a new life in another sphere of existence.

If the funeral is in part to help the bereaved face the reality and finality of death (van Gennep's pre-liminal stage) then it is important that the language we use does not constantly seek to deny that reality. The instinct of pastors is to want to soften blows: so we speak of 'falling asleep' rather than dying. The language of the liturgy, at any rate, is robust and to the point.

Making the transition

In the second place, the funeral service is a *rite de passage* for the bereaved. The settled pattern of their lives has been severely disrupted – a loved one has died – and this has plunged them into turmoil. The service has to acknowledge this dislocation and the sorrow and pain which it brings, while helping the bereaved to make sense of what has happened and begin to relate to the deceased in a new way.

There are two moments in the service where this transition is highlighted. First, there is the address. Although *Common Worship* allows for the possibility of both a tribute and a sermon, the reality of most 25-minute funerals is that the address must encompass both. The address will generally have three elements to it:

Thanksgiving for the life of the deceased – though avoiding idealistic eulogy.
Some setting of this death within the wider context of human mortality and the Christian hope.
An acknowledgement of the bereaved and their needs.

The minister will speak about the bereaved, the loss they have sustained and the support they will need from family, friends and the wider community as they pick up the threads of their lives again. There is a brief opportunity to make it clear that their relationship with their loved one is now changed by death but not lost. They have their memories, painful now, but over time they may become a source of gratitude and comfort. They can also be close to their loved one at particular places – the grave, this church, in favourite spots – and in prayer. (The letter I leave with the bereaved includes a prayer which they can say for themselves. See Appendix 1.)

We are tempted to say to mourners that 'time heals', but we need to be clear that without further explanation this may be heard in two quite different ways, only one of which is helpful. It can give the impression that over time we forget our loved ones, that they cease to be important to us because they are no longer at the forefront of our day-to-day concerns. (See Karen's story, 'Grieving for a baby in 1972', at the end of Chapter 5.) While this might be true, it is hardly a source of comfort in the context of early grieving. Rather, we need to make it clear that 'time heals' in the sense that over time we learn to relate to our dead in new ways, ways which do not cause us as much pain as this initial separation has done.

As well as helping the bereaved to begin to find a new way of relating to the dead, the funeral also helps them to find new ways of relating to the living – to those within the family as well as those in the wider community. For the bereaved are now no longer wife but widow, no longer husband but widower, no longer oldest son but oldest member of this family. The ritual of the funeral can help to make clear the profound transformation that this death means for those loved ones who are left and so help them begin to make the transition to their new familial or social status.

A second moment where the needs of the bereaved come more sharply into focus is during the intercessions. Whatever form these take it is always important to pray appropriately for those who mourn. The newer forms of service, such as *Common Worship*, are a much richer resource in this respect than older forms. We have noted in an earlier chapter that the Book of Common Prayer rather assumes that the only help mourners need is to be reminded of the resurrection hope. *Common Worship* recognizes that people are bereaved in many different circumstances and this needs to be acknowledged in prayer appropriately. So, for example, a bereaved person may be mourning the loss of a first baby or a partner of fifty years. *Common Worship* also recognizes that people experience different emotions at a time of death. They may feel profoundly sad; death may strike them as cruel and unfair. They may feel considerable relief after nursing their loved one through a long and painful illness; death seems a merciful release. They may be feeling guilty because they had a row with their partner shortly before he had his fatal heart attack. They may be feeling utterly bewildered in the face of a suicide, or very angry after death at the hands of a drunk driver. They may, of course, experience a strange mix of conflicting emotions. Prayers appropriately chosen can help the bereaved to come to terms with the particular circumstances of the death and the emotions it has triggered. The right words can help those who mourn to realize that their feelings are not unusual or out of place.

The funeral service enables all who mourn to make sense of this senseless occurrence – the death of someone loved and cared about – by setting the event in the wider perspective which the

Christian faith gives. It provides what some psychologists would call a 'core percept' – a key idea around which other notions can be organized: for example, the Christian faith teaches us that God can bring life out of death and we are in his care whether we live or die. This is the core message of the whole of the rite even though it may only be articulated in that form in one or two places.

Reincorporation into society

A third aspect of the funeral service is related to what van Gennep calls post-liminal – the reincorporation of the bereaved into society. This is not something that can be accomplished quickly, certainly not by the end of a funeral service! But in the service – in the prayers and the preaching – indications can be given as to how this is to be achieved. In the prayers we pray for the bereaved in the coming days, that they may find strength from God and from family, from close friends and from the community. In the address, the minister can remind the wider congregation of friends and neighbours that they can help the bereaved find a place again in the life of the community. It will not be quite as before because now they will not have their loved one with them. They need friends who are sensitive to what they will feel for perhaps a long time; friends who will not overwhelm them, or force the pace, but who, on the other hand, will not simply forget them once the funeral is over.

The follow-up

Ministers need to be realistic about what they can and cannot offer personally by way of follow-up. It may be possible to make one further call, say, one week after the funeral service. But even this modest goal may prove difficult in a busy parish. Ministers, therefore, have to be discriminating in when they do or do not call again; they should not give the impression that they will call and then fail to do so. Most people will work through their grief with the help of family and good friends and with their own resources. But a few will need on-going help for a while. Perhaps a more satisfactory way of offering care after the funeral to those that need it is to build a team of lay visitors who can make what follow-up calls seem appropriate. (See the suggestion for a

Magdalene Group in Appendix 2.) The minister can also make it clear – in the letter left at the pre-funeral visit – that if the bereaved need more help in the future they only have to make a telephone call.

There is one way in which further contact can be maintained without overburdening the pastor or raising unrealistic expectations amongst the bereaved. An annual memorial service can be held, perhaps on Easter Day or at All Souls-tide, when all those who died in the previous year are remembered by name and others on request. Once established the numbers attending such a service will witness to its pastoral effectiveness.

Conclusion

For many years now the majority of weddings in Britain have not been solemnized in churches. A range of attractive alternatives has been provided, in hotels and country clubs and elsewhere. In the process, any religious dimension has been lost, and since many of these marriages have been held at a considerable distance from the local community, that has inevitably made them less of a community and more a private celebration as well. These trends are set to continue. This has not wholly happened to the funeral, but it will if those who currently conduct funerals and offer pastoral care on behalf of the churches do not recognize and respond to the trends I have outlined. Does this matter? Only if you think that the further secularization and privatization of death does not serve either individuals or society well.

People grieve in many different ways

The inexperienced pastor can easily assume that if emotion is not shown it is not felt, and conversely, that if it is shown it must run deep. As a young vicar I learnt the hard way and Mr Masarella was one of those who helped me.

When I reached the house, a neighbour of Mr and Mrs Masarella met me at the door. She warned me that Mr Masarella was in the sitting room clinging to the dead body of his wife and was quite inconsolable. It was as she described. Elizabeth Masarella – a woman in her middle fifties – lay under the front room window on a single bed that had been brought downstairs during the final stages of her cancer. She was a big woman and looked for all the world like the dead heroine in an Italian opera. Her husband, Tony, was holding one of her hands against his chest, crying and calling out in a mixture of English and Italian. When he saw me he began to wail even more loudly. 'What am I going to do? Mama is dead. What am I going to do? My wife, my beautiful wife, is dead? How can I go on living without my bellissima...'

I sympathized and tried to get him to talk about the funeral service which had been arranged by the funeral director in two days' time. But each time I asked a question he broke down again and cried and wailed all the more. After half an hour of this it was obvious that I was not going to get any questions answered that day. I said I would call the following morning. But when I did so, the same pattern was repeated. Fortunately, the neighbour was able to give me the telephone number of one of their adult children who helped me to construct some outline of Mrs Masarella's life – she was English, he was Italian – and gave me some idea as to her character...

The funeral service went relatively smoothly as long as you ignored Mr Masarella's loud sobs and occasional shouts in Italian. But at the graveside he became quite distraught. He sobbed, he called out. He collapsed into the arms of his son. Finally he fell on his hands and knees at the edge of the grave calling down to his dead wife. Then suddenly he jumped into the grave and fell on the top of the coffin. There was a long delay while he was pulled out by the funeral director's men. By this time almost the entire funeral party was sobbing and holding their hands out towards Mr Masarella.

After the service we went to a local public house where sandwiches had been laid on. Mr Masarella sat utterly disconsolate in a corner, eating nothing, and breaking down again each time someone came up to express condolences...

I returned home that evening very disturbed and resolved to call on Mr Masarella the next day. I was met by a neighbour who told me that he had gone away to stay with relatives in the south of England...

A couple of months later, as I was walking down the main shopping street in the parish, I heard a familiar voice calling out to me, 'Hi, Father. It's me, Tony.' I turned and saw Mr Masarella walking along with his arm firmly wrapped around a smartly dressed youngish woman. 'Father, I want you to meet the happiest man in the world. And the woman who has made me happy. This is my cousin. We want you to marry us in a few months.'

And I did.

What conclusions did I draw from this? Two. First, we should not necessarily equate depth of feeling with the degree to which it is expressed. Some people find some release from the pain of loss from an effusive expression of their feelings. Others cope differently. Second, there is a type of man (usually a man) who simply cannot live on his own. However devoted he may have been to his wife, after her death we should never be surprised to find him with a new partner sooner rather than later. There is no insincerity here; this is simply how some people are.

Questions

1. A funeral is for the living not the dead. How far do you agree?
2. Does the funeral liturgy say enough about the Christian hope without some expression of that hope in a sermon?
3. How far should views which are alien to Christianity be allowed expression in a funeral service?
4. What does a minister say if asked to take the funeral of an avowed non-believer?

~8~

Good grief

Pastoral care of the bereaved

Everyday I find it harder to bear. For what point is there in life now?
Dora Carrington, *Diaries*

When my father died I did not cry at all.
Simone de Beauvoir, *A Very Easy Death*

Introduction

The way human beings express their grief when a loved one dies varies from culture to culture and has changed over time. At the time of Jesus, for example, there seems to have been a tradition of very public wailing in the Jewish community when someone died.[1] Yet we also know that in the same period among the Greeks, those influenced by Stoicism sought to restrain any overt emotional display. Christians have sometimes regarded weeping as a natural sign of genuine affection; but at other times it has been seen as a lack of faith and has been discouraged. Yet despite the fact that any examination of the past quickly reveals the part that social factors play in grieving, during the course of the twentieth century the social insights of sociologists such as Emile Durkheim have generally been overlooked. We have turned almost exclusively to the psychologists to inform our understanding of grief.

Durkheim believed that the intensity or otherwise of grieving was dependent not on any innate, universal feelings but on the degree to which society valued some categories of people rather than others. So, for example, in the early part of the last century the death of small babies created less emotion than the death of middle-aged fathers or mothers. This was because the death of children was not uncommon and children – unlike fathers and mothers – had not had time to create networks of significant relationships or make any particular contribution to the wider community. But by the beginning of the present century the death of babies was an occasion for very great grief. When, for instance, the baby daughter of the Chancellor of the Exchequer died in January 2002, one sober political commentator, not usually given to exaggeration, felt constrained to write, 'But there is no form of bereavement as bad as the loss of a child... '[2] Really? Not even the loss of a partner of twenty-five years? We can, however, see the kind of social changes during the course of the last century that led to this change in intensity of grieving for a baby. With better health care, the death of babies had become a relatively rare event; easily available contraceptives meant that most births were now planned; professional people put off having children until later in their lives and careers. Consequently, the arrival of a baby now marked the fulfilment of hopes and plans nurtured carefully over a long time. It was invested with very great significance and as a result occasioned greater grief than at other periods in history, including quite recent history. But the point is that the intensity of grief is not a universal given but in large part the consequence of wider social factors that continually change.

All of this has implications for what is regarded as 'normal' and 'abnormal' grief. In our society it would be abnormal to be inconsolable over the death of a frail, elderly parent who had lived a long life, but not over the death of a child. There are also socially suggested gender differences: what is or is not appropriate behaviour for men and women varies. Men are expected to be more stoical, and often are; women are expected to be more overtly emotional, and often are – though under the influence of the counselling movement it is 'all right' for men to show some emotion. This is because grieving is part of wider patterns of gendered behaviour. We can see this illustrated in this brief extract from some autobiographical writing of the author Jan Morris. She had begun life as James Morris, at one point climbing Everest with Sir Edmund Hillary, but after a sex change operation, she noted how reactions and expectations – her own as well as other people's – changed as well:

> It amuses me to consider, for instance, when I am taken out to lunch by one of my more urbane men friends, that not so many years ago that fulsome waiter would have treated me as he is now treating him. Then he would have greeted me with respectful seriousness. Now he unfolds my napkin with a playful flourish, as if to humour me. Then he would have taken my order with grave concern, now he expects me to say something frivolous (and I do).[3]

And I do. We may think we are behaving spontaneously; we are often acting out a role.

Grieving is also shaped by the way we understand death and make sense of it. Here the prevailing assumptions of the dominant culture are not always reflected in particular subcultures. Among Hindus, for instance, too much weeping at a death is frowned upon. It can create a river that the soul has to surmount. Normal grief would then be stoical and abnormal grief would be more effusive – the reverse of what much contemporary counselling theory has suggested. It is considerations like this that make counselling a hazardous task if counsellors are not familiar with cultural diversity.

But, as we saw in Chapter 4, by the middle of the twentieth century, as religion ceased to play a significant role in the lives of most British people, even at the time of death, grieving had come to be discussed almost exclusively in terms of individual emotional experience. Grieving has been individualized and psychologized, divorced from any social setting, to be treated medically. In such a situation, a role could be found for the doctor (and later the counsellor) but not the minister of religion.

In Britain today few Christian communities are so bounded that they can resist the general patterns of mourning and grieving in contemporary society. Membership of a Christian community adds some components – it may help to provide meaning and a supportive group – but Christians are as influenced by the prevailing features of the culture as anyone else. As we have already seen, these are: the decline of community mourning; the privatization of grief; the broad acceptance that grief is better dealt with when expressed; and the idea that grieving is a psychological process through which the bereaved passes over a period of time. There is likely to be little difference, therefore, in the experiences of people because they are members of a church, unless that church has clear and consistent teaching about death and well-understood practices at the time of death. There is an issue here for theologically liberal churches.

There is one further aspect to grieving in contemporary society. Since people now generally live longer and die of degenerative diseases taking their course rather than suddenly, many people find themselves caring for a dying loved one over a long period of time. This can mean that the process of adjusting to a death, bereavement, begins before the death itself. When death occurs, the bereaved are sorrowful but not necessarily overwhelmed with emotion. It can also mean that the initial reaction to the death may be one not of sorrow but of relief – that the suffering is ended and the burden of caring lifted – and this can sometimes make people feel wretched and guilty. The sensitive pastor will help people to explore these strange and often contradictory feelings.

Aspects of grief

Before turning specifically to the role of the pastor let us consider first the psychological states which grieving people may experience. This is not to say that everyone will have all of these experiences or that they will have them in this sequence or that these experiences are universal, since we are mindful of the social factors which shape grieving and its intensity. But knowing what psychologists have discovered helps the minister to be sensitive to what he may encounter. Psychology can be a useful servant though a tyrannous master. I find it more helpful to think in terms of 'aspects' of grief than 'stages' of grief or even 'components'. Stages suggest a certain process and sequence – and the one thing a pastor comes to know is that there are no 'stages' through which everyone does or must pass.[4] The term 'components' draws attention to the variety of emotions which people may feel and does not suggest any necessary sequence, though the final component – reintegration – is understood as the desired goal of the grieving process.[5] But 'aspects' simply alerts the pastor to the fact that grieving people may experience a range of emotions in no particular order and with no suggestion that there should be a common goal for the bereaved beyond saying that we want to enable grieving people to live their lives as well as they can.

Shock

Many bereaved people speak first of their sense of profound shock when their loved one dies. The less expected the death and the closer the bond with the dead, the greater the shock. Suddenly everything seems unreal. It is as if they were in a dream. They may experience a variety of sensations: calmness can give way to panic, panic can lead to apathy and an inability to do anything. These mental states may be accompanied by various physical sensations such as pain, tightness in the chest, or breathing difficulties.

People in shock often find quite simple tasks very difficult. Opening the mail may seem an insuperable and pointless task. They cannot make the effort to see friends. They lose all track of time passing. One day seems like any other. They cannot prepare or eat food – even though they know they should eat. People in shock who stop eating can quickly lose weight – and this may be a key indicator of the need for further support.

Disorganization

Some bereaved people find it helpful to have many tasks that have to be accomplished immediately after the death. The death certificate may have to be collected, the death must be registered, the funeral director has to be informed and the funeral planned. There may be visits to doctors, to registrars, to solicitors, to banks and building societies, to funeral directors, to relatives. They can keep going until after the funeral. But other people find they cannot do any of these things. In fact, as we have noted, they cannot perform even the simplest of tasks. Everything becomes a burden and a mountain to climb.

Denial

Denial is a psychological mechanism which only gives cause for alarm if it persists over a long time. For a short time it seems that some people can only come to terms with a devastating loss by behaving as if their loved one were not really dead at all. I visited one woman who continued to lay a place for her husband at the dinner table for several weeks after his death. She explained it to me in this way: 'Even during the funeral service I thought at the back of my mind, "Perhaps there has been a mistake." I didn't want to do anything that killed off that possibility.' In the end she accepted the reality of his death and simply stopped putting out his knife and fork. But she needed more time to accept the reality of the situation than our brief contemporary funeral rites allow.

Sometimes bereaved people have a strong sense of the presence of the dead with them. This may persist for some time, but does gradually fade. It only becomes denial if the bereaved treat these experiences as somehow contradicting the reality of the death. Pastors generally do not need to confront people directly, though they should not collude with denial.

The idea of denial is now widely used but may be applied unwisely. One woman told me that after her young daughter died in a road accident she kept her bedroom as it had been when the child was alive and each evening went into the room to sit and think about her. After several months her husband and other members of the family became very angry and said she was in denial. She said it was her way of remembering her daughter whose death she completely accepted. Very reluctantly she allowed the members of the family to reorder the room and remove all trace of her daughter. I was left wondering who was doing the denying.

Relief

One of the more important pastoral tasks is to allow the bereaved to speak honestly and openly about their feelings. People may be reluctant to admit to relatives that they felt an overwhelming sense of relief. But if you have nursed someone over a long period, or watched a loved one suffer, you may well feel relief that the watching and the waiting and the caring are now at an end. Occasionally, carers who feel relief sometimes also feel lost in that the central meaning of their life – caring for a sick wife – has suddenly been taken away.

Some years ago I took the funeral of a toddler who had been suffocated when a pile of sand in which he had been playing collapsed on him. I asked his mother how she felt. She said, 'I have a huge sense of relief, and I feel bad about it.' As we examined this we came to the conclusion that parents, and especially the principal carer, carry with them at every moment the burden of responsibility for their small children. They have to think about them all the time and guard against any number of things that may happen to them during the course of an average day. 'I realized that I didn't have to worry about Zack any more.' But that can quickly lead to feelings of guilt if it is not understood.

Occasionally the bereaved come to see that life with their partner had become unhappy, lonely or oppressive. The realization that this was so had been either suppressed or scarcely admitted: daily life had to be got through. But now the partner is dead and the sense of relief palpable. This may not be incompatible with feelings of sadness. There is nothing to say that we cannot experience contradictory emotions just as we entertain contradictory opinions. The task of the pastor is to help people recognize and acknowledge the feelings and deal with them appropriately.

Guilt

A death will often trigger feelings of guilt, both rational and irrational. Children who have neglected elderly parents can suddenly feel bad about it. Even conscientious ones can feel that they ought to have done more. Failure to be with a loved one at the moment of death can also create guilt. It is as if all the caring that had gone before now counted for less because one had failed them at the last moment. Since most people continue to die in hospital and relatives may not be there in time this is a common reaction.

Pastors need to be aware of the possibilities of guilt in two particular circumstances. The more obvious is where the deceased has taken their own life. People may be very hard on themselves as they struggle with all the questions that come, often unbidden, into the mind: Why didn't we notice? What did we do that drove him to this? Were we such bad parents that he couldn't even share his worries with us?

The death of young people may create feelings of guilt in siblings. They may feel, rationally or irrationally, that they have been unkind or unloving. If their brother or sister has been ill over a period of years they may have resented the time and attention that was devoted to them, and the lack of attention they believed they had. Now they experience guilt for harbouring such thoughts and feelings even if they never articulated them. One 12-year-old told me that she had wished her brother was dead because she wanted his room. Now he was dead it was as if she had killed him even though he died of cancer. She could not allow herself to have his room.

We should not seek to squash the expression of these feelings but rather let the bereaved talk about them. As we talk we can begin to distinguish feelings which may reflect real situations and those which do not. The former may need to be 'confessed'; the latter need to be seen in an altogether different light.

Depression

Most people will probably experience depression at some moments even if only in a minor form. It is a sign that we are coming to terms with the situation of loss, a recognition that we are powerless to change what has happened. For a while we dwell on what we have lost and cannot begin to think about the future as anything other than a future without the loved one. It may take the form of profound emptiness and yearning, perhaps combined with moments of sharper pain. It may also be more acute with feelings of desperation and hopelessness.

The pastor will want to emphasize the normality of the experience and must be prepared to spend some time hearing the same or similar stories many times. This is to be expected since your world is being turned upside-down. If it becomes unbearable then the doctor should be informed. But many will not want or need to resort to pills if they know that the black periods do come to an end or subside. However, we should resist the temptation of telling the bereaved what may be untrue for them – that time heals. It is hard, however, for the pastor not to be affected by deep sadness. Bereavement visiting drains energy, and those who minister to the bereaved need to recognize their own need to replenish those drained resources.

Anger

Bereaved people who lose loved ones they were especially close to may find themselves with deep feelings of anger. This may take the form of anger at nothing and nobody in particular, or it may be focused – on the doctors who were uncaring, on other relatives who didn't do enough or are not grieving appropriately, on God who allowed it, on the minister as God's representative, or even on the deceased: why did they let me down?

For a while, mind and body may cope by withdrawing from the world, taking no interest in matters beyond the home, retreating into the family or among close friends. This is helpful in the initial period of coming to terms with the loss but it is not a permanent solution: reality has to be re-engaged. There is a particular problem when a husband and wife are bereaved through the death of a child. Each grieves in their own way – which may not be the way of the partner; and each needs support – which the other may not be able to give, or to give as much as the other might like. This can result in anger.

Pastors need to make it clear that anger is a perfectly proper emotion for people to feel in the presence of God. We can be angry, even angry with God, and still pray, 'Nevertheless I am continually with thee; thou dost hold my right hand... Whom have I in heaven but thee?'[6] (Psalms of 'disorientation' – such as this one – may be a very helpful resource on these occasions.[7])

Anxiety

Attacks of anxiety, severe or mild, occur as people begin to contemplate how their familiar world has been turned upside-down and they were powerless to do anything about it. Perhaps there are many areas of their lives over which they may now be about to lose control. They may fear losing control over their emotions. Death may plunge someone into depths of feeling that they have scarcely known before – and they cannot mitigate the effects by any act of will. They may fear losing control over their future: how can I cope without my husband, my wife? Worries increase if there are dependent children or a house goes with a job or a drop in income is feared. Established roles within a family or community are now changed: no longer a wife but a widow.

Resolution and re-establishment

Eventually the death of a loved one is accepted and all attempts at denial are laid aside. The world has changed permanently and that is now understood. The funeral plays an important role in this part of the process. The lowering of the coffin into the grave or the disappearance behind the crematorium curtain signifies finality and closure. The dead are dead and they will not be seen again. Now the work of reordering one's life without the bodily presence of the other person begins. It may be a slow process and there will be many returns to previous states of anxiety or depression or anger. But over time, for most people, the raw wounds of grief close and heal over, opening up again at particularly poignant moments – a first anniversary, Christmas Day, a birthday – or when something suddenly reminds the bereaved of the one who has died.

Should this be called 'letting go' – as the literature usually suggests? This may be too stark a way of describing what happens in bereavement, at least for some. It suggests that there can be no continuing relationship with the dead that can endure over time. Let go and move on. Some of the earlier writing in the twentieth century, no doubt reacting against Victorian sentimentality, did seem to suggest that this was how it must be: the goal of bereavement must be to lead to the breaking of affective bonds. This seems to have been Freud's view and it can still be found in some of the counselling literature.[8] It is a view which is congruent with both a more secular age, suspicious of raising (false) hopes of immortality, and traditional forms of Protestantism, which has always discouraged any attempt to continue a relationship with the dead – as in prayers for the dead. It may also reflect patterns of behaviour in men. Men – whether for reasons of culture or biology or both – seem more inclined to let go and move on. Women seem to want to maintain bonds with their dead loved ones.

But must there be a severing of the bonds with the dead even if we reject the notion of life after death? Tony Walter has suggested that what the bereaved may learn is – to use a Freudian term – to internalize the dead. As we let go of our loved ones we also form pictures and impressions of them which can give us solace and joy for the rest of our lives.[9] This point of view seems to be gaining more general acceptance among counsellors, many of whom are women. Of course, most of the public probably never doubted it but they were made to feel wretched because they could not or would not 'let go' their dead. For some, the very idea of 'resolution' appals. It suggests that they should forget or cease to feel deep affection for their loved ones.

For those who have jobs to go to, returning to work means that they have to come to terms with a death and re-engage with the wider society more quickly than they otherwise might. At one time this would have meant a division between men and women. Gender differences may still be a factor but increasingly women are also in employment. While this swift return to doing normal things may help many if not most, some find it hard to have to put on a brave face and may feel that they have not had enough time to make adjustments. Pastors should be sensitive to the needs of those who work and give the impression that they are reintegrated.

Christian congregations are one of the places where the bereaved, the widow or the widower, can build a social life again without a partner. Congregations often have within them people who have gone through the experience of bereavement and who understand the difficulties. We should not underestimate the role a congregation can play.

Loneliness

I have put 'loneliness' after 'resolution' to make the point that some people never do 'get over' the death of someone close. They continue to experience a deep sense of loneliness which persists for a very long time if not for the rest of their life. This is not some generalized lack of companionship but a longing for a particular person, the deceased. Nor is it simply a matter of establishing a new identity which is not dependent on being part of a pair, though this will be a factor. But for a few people there never can be a substitute for the one who has died because that relationship was one of such intimacy and depth. The pastor may be one of the few people who is willing to say, 'You may be right. Time does not always heal.'

The needs of the bereaved and the role of the pastor

Colin Murray Parkes has pointed out that what happens to a person when a loved one dies is that their entire internal world of assumptions collapses. From waking up in the morning to going to bed at night what we had come to expect as normal is no longer the case. There is no one else brushing their teeth alongside us, there is no need to set out two places for lunch and dinner, there is no one to consult about a letter from the town council, there is an empty bed to get into at the end of the day. In almost every aspect of daily life this 'assumptive world' has been drastically changed, and we are powerless to affect it.[10] Moreover, these assumptions are not simply about what we believe and think, they also underlie a large number of the habits and patterns of behaviour that make up our day-to-day lives. The hardest feature of all may be that the one to whom one would normally turn for advice and comfort is the one who is dead.

The world we knew so well and were so at home in suddenly becomes an unfamiliar place. If the bereaved are to learn to live in this unfamiliar world they need to make a number of adjustments and in order to do that they need a good deal of emotional support. Some of this support may come from the doctor – though the focus of the medical profession is on scientific medicine rather than the pastoral care of the bereaved – but normally it will come from the family. The minister has privileged access for a short period around the time of the funeral, or longer if the family is part of his congregation.

The extent of a person's reaction to a death probably depends more on the depth of the attachment in life than the nature of the relationship. The death of a spouse may be devastating, though some spouses have long since fallen out of love and coexist rather than relate intimately. But the death of a child may be more traumatic for a parent that has formed a strong emotional bond. Death may reveal depths of attachment which those outside of the relationship were not fully aware of. We have already seen that social factors are at work here. In a society which places great value on marriage as partnership, as ours does, the death of a spouse may be felt intensely.

The bereaved have three particular needs.

Accepting the reality

The first need of the recently bereaved is to be able to accept the reality of the death. One way in which this is accomplished is by allowing the bereaved to talk about their loved ones – endlessly and in the past tense. Sometimes family members think this is maudlin and seek to stop it. The bereaved themselves may suspect what others are thinking and keep quiet voluntarily. But the pastor can encourage it. He begins the process at the pre-funeral visit as he takes notes for a tribute in the service. This should not be rushed. After the funeral the need to talk remains and is generally taken up by family and friends, but a return visit by the minister or a bereavement visiting team may be particularly valuable where family and friends find it tedious to go over the same ground again and again. Once more we find that time and a willingness to listen may be the key pastoral gifts. In a society where mourning – ritualized ways of coping with grief – has been vastly reduced, the need for good listeners has correspondingly increased.

Accepting the pain

The natural inclination of relatives is to try to shield the bereaved from the pain of loss – and in doing so shield themselves from it as well. They may do this by arranging various distractions, designed to 'take mum's mind off things'. Or they may suggest asking the doctor for more tranquillizers. Or they may try to encourage a rather forced cheerfulness. But it is important that the bereaved wrestle with the sadness and the pain, otherwise they may lie hidden until some future event triggers them into irrational life. The pastor stands outside the immediate circle, yet is accepted within it, and so can help the bereaved to face the pain of loss. He will suggest that what the bereaved is feeling is quite normal, that they are not going mad or losing control. They have been hurt and the wound is deep and will take time to heal. It may never heal completely, but in time it will heal enough for them to live their lives again, even though the quality of their life has been significantly affected.

Accepting the changed situation and the new role of the dead

Whatever the circumstances of the bereaved person, those circumstances will have been changed in some way by the death of their loved one. They may now find themselves alone for the first time in their lives. They may find themselves the sole parent of children. They may find themselves having to do all the domestic chores that were once undertaken by a partner. The list goes on. The pastoral task is to help the bereaved think about the changed situation and what it entails.

There is also the part that the dead are going to have in the on-going life of the bereaved. We have already noted that in putting the emphasis here – on a continuing role – we are moving away from an earlier understanding of grieving which spoke about the need to 'let go' the dead: in other words, as far as possible, to forget them. This is what lies behind these sorts of comments: 'You are young enough to marry again' – to a man in his early forties whose wife had recently died of cancer; 'When your new baby comes you will feel different' – to a pregnant woman who still cried most days remembering her first baby who died after a few days of life; 'Time will heal' – said to everybody. The comments are generally said with kindness but they fall like hammer blows on those who do not accept that 'letting go', accommodating, forgetting, is a desirable end of grieving.

The dead can play two sorts of role in the on-going life of the bereaved. They can continue to exercise an influence as if they were still alive and this can be unhelpful as the bereaved seek to adjust to their new life. So, for example, a man may feel inhibited from beginning a friendship with a woman because he feels this may be disloyal to his dead wife. Or they can be a source of support and comfort through the recalling of good or happy or challenging memories.

The newly bereaved can think that their dead loved ones have ceased to play a role in their lives, that they have been abandoned by them. This need not be so and the pastoral task is to help the bereaved see what that new role is, which is about locating good memories in the on-going life of the bereaved. If well-meaning relatives and friends try to discourage the bereaved from 'dwelling on the past' or 'getting morbid', the pastor can help them see why this recollection is important. It is neither dwelling on nor in the past but integrating the dead loved one into the on-going life of the bereaved.

The church community plays a role here too through its record of the dead. The annual recollection of the faithful departed in prayer can be a continuing source of comfort. This can be done at the Sunday service or at a special annual service – for instance at All Souls (2 November) or Eastertide. As well as reading out the names of the dead, congregations might be encouraged to bring a photograph or some piece of memorabilia for everyone present to see and share. In this way the church helps the dead to have an on-going relationship with not just the immediate family but the wider Christian community as well.

For most people the passage of time will dull the pain of separation and loss. Though not for all. Whereas for most people there seem to be limits to the body's capacity to go on feeling pain at a certain level, for a few, the later memories are recalled with just as much sadness and sharpness. Much depends on whether the bereaved are able to find new patterns of relationships in their altered circumstances, and here a Christian community has a role to play.

It is very unlikely that the pastor can visit the bereaved who need contact on a frequent basis for very long, though it is worth remembering that there may be few other professionals around with either the time or the skill to help. An important part of the pastoral task of the clergy, therefore, is to build up pastorally minded congregations from whom bereavement visiting teams can be formed. It is particularly helpful to the bereaved if the person who visits them has had first-hand knowledge of bereavement, especially of the kind they have suffered. It is important for these lay teams to realize that they are not offering counselling. The techniques are quite different. In counselling the counsellor remains detached, an external observer, seemingly untouched by the emotions generated by the death. They proceed by gently putting questions to the bereaved about their feelings and seek to help the bereaved understand their responses. But the lay visitor proceeds more by way of conversation, as a friend would. As with a friend, it is more reassuring if they can express something of their own feelings rather than appear unmoved – though they should be careful not to burden the bereaved further. One of the complaints of more formal counselling by the bereaved is that the counsellor can seem detached.

Conclusion

As we move further into the twenty-first century we can expect all those features of the post-traditional world which we have identified throughout these chapters to continue to play an important role in deciding the shape of grief in British society. Organized religion may decline further, but spirituality, within and without the churches, will continue to grow. There is both sacralization and secularization at work. The Christian minister represents the love and support of a Christian congregation. He must also seek to interpret what is happening to the bereaved in the light of the Christian faith and in ways which strike chords in the bereaved. The task is more demanding in a world which no longer accepts there is or ever could be one overarching canopy of sacred beliefs which can illuminate everything. The minister needs to have broad sympathy and his wits about him.

Coping

These are two more recent instances of bereavement. They show us that what comforts people will vary enormously from person to person. Pastors need to be sensitive to what may be helpful in a particular case.

Ted was a loving father and grandfather, but neither he nor any member of his family had any connection with the church. He was also a member of a Dixieland jazz band. He lived for his music and it was through the band that he had made so many friends. His wife asked rather gingerly whether some of the band might be allowed to play a little music as we left the church. It soon became apparent that whatever I might say in an address about his love of jazz, some music by his band would be many times more eloquent in calling Ted to mind. So I phoned the band leader.

We agreed two things. First, the members of the band would write down a sentence or two about Ted – how they might remember him and what he meant to them. These words I would incorporate in the tribute to him. Second, we decided that we would play Ted in and out New Orleans-style.

On the day of the funeral the church quickly filled with friends and colleagues. The members of a 12-piece band gradually assembled and played a medley of pieces before the service began. Then as the coffin was carried in and the words, 'I am the resurrection and the life' rang out, they began to play in slow time 'Rock of ages'.

When I came to the address and drew on the words which band members had supplied, I was immediately aware that every word I said about Ted evoked him in the minds of the congregation. There was a great deal of weeping, cheerful yet sad.

At the end, as we began to move out, the band struck up 'When the saints go marching in' at a furious pace.

The following Sunday Ted's widow came to church with her family. The following Sunday she came again on her own. She had found the service very moving and she now found the church a place of real comfort. It brought back good memories of the funeral and so of Ted. More than this, it enabled her at these moments to feel close to him again. She explained it in this way: 'I don't think of him as being with me like a ghost or anything. It's not frightening. I just feel him with me. And I can sort of love him still. Though I don't think I could tell Anthony [her son] about it.'

***

Gwen Jones was inconsolable at her husband's funeral, so I resolved to go and see her about a week later. I found her at home in the kitchen. She invited me to sit down at the kitchen table while she made a pot of tea. As she prepared the tea she took a small plastic lunch box from the table and emptied the contents into the waste bin. 'Danny's snap', she explained. Danny was her late husband. She went on: 'I make his sandwiches up every day for work as usual, but he doesn't take them, of course. So I throw them away again every afternoon.'

For a while I was troubled by this. I cast around in my mind for an explanation. Was it denial, an inability or unwillingness to come to terms with her husband's death? Not really, for she seemed to acknowledge he was dead. Rather, it was a continuation for the moment of older patterns of living before new ones had had a chance to be formed. This is what she had done every working day for twenty years. She was not going to disrupt the pattern of her daily life just like that because he had died, even though it made no sense to prepare a lunch box for a man who was never going to eat it. Even so, I knew that such behaviour might become pathological, or perhaps already was. I resolved to go back again the following week… .

Gwen was in her kitchen again. I accepted another cup of tea and she caught me looking around the room. 'Were you looking for the sandwiches?' she asked. I had to confess. She laughed. 'I don't do it any more. I woke up one morning and said, Come on, old girl, it's time you bucked your ideas up. There's the rest of your life. So I stopped doing the sandwiches. But, and don't laugh, vicar, sometimes I do them again, just to feel close to him. Silly, isn't it?'

Questions

1. If funerals are for the living not the dead, what elements of a service would bring most comfort?
2. If a bereaved person shows no overt signs of grieving should we worry?
3. What qualities would you look for in a member of a bereavement visiting group?
4. How much of being a pastor can be taught?

Afterword

There is no such thing as a natural death: nothing that happens to a man is ever natural since his presence calls the world into question.
Simone de Beauvoir

The completely secular funeral is a rare event in contemporary Britain. Clergy continue to provide pastoral ministry at the time of death for the majority of people, and growing numbers of Christian lay people are involved in caring for the bereaved. On the face of it, this makes little sense if we are living in a culture in which religion has been pushed to the margins. How do we explain it?

I have suggested that while most people have largely turned their back on organized religion they have not embraced wholeheartedly the secular (medical) definition of death which seems to reduce their experience. A religious (Christian) understanding of death has not been wholly lost or given up. This is why people are still willing for ministers of religion to conduct funerals: they are not persuaded that death is the last word on human life.

In this situation, there remain opportunities for pastors, lay and ordained, to speak about the Christian understanding: that is a vital part of ministry. In a plural culture, however, that has to be done with greater awareness of alternative perspectives; we cannot shut down debate even if we wanted to. This suggests a more exploratory than didactic approach by ministers.

Yet it is hard for Christians, clerical and lay, after centuries of wanting to exercise control over key aspects of people's lives, to adapt to the quite different role of helping people explore their experience, albeit using the Christian faith as a key resource. The temptation is to not even try, but to take another path altogether, seeking social usefulness by adopting some secular model of pastoral care – as a counsellor, for instance – and ducking the religious questions. We need to be more confident in assuming a role as Christian pastors.

However, as the twenty-first century unfolds, those to whom we minister will listen to us only in so far as we are willing to engage with them in a genuine exploration of their experiences of dying and bereavement. Yes, we have our Christian faith to guide and encourage us: God is the God of the living, not the dead, and he has called us to enjoy his friendship in heaven. But no, we do not have all the answers.

Appendix 1

This is an example of a proforma letter which can be completed during the pre-funeral visit and left with the bereaved by the minister. It gives them basic information which they may not have fully taken in during the visit. It also gives the name of the minister and a way of contacting the minister should the need arise.

St Lucy's Church, Newtown

Vicar: The Revd Jane Green, The Vicarage,
Vicarage Road, Newtown. Tel. 123654
Curate: The Revd John Brown, 6 The Court,
Newtown. Tel. 321456
Readers: Maggie Black. Tel. 412536,
Arthur Gray. Tel. 654123

Dear

I called to say I was sorry to hear your news and to assure you that we shall do everything we can to help you at this time. I set out below what we have so far agreed about the service. If you want to change anything or add to this, please give me a ring. I am usually at home in the mornings or in the evening between 5 and 7 p.m.

Date, time and place of service:

Requests (readings/music/hymns):

I expect you feel rather numb at present, but later you might find the reading and prayer below helpful. If I can help in any other way, either now or in the future, please do not hesitate to contact me, the curate or reader.

Yours sincerely

Notes

- We shall remember .... by name in the service on Sunday at 10 a.m. (Sung Eucharist). You would be most welcome to come if that would help you. We also remember all those who have died each year on Easter Sunday at a special service at 3 p.m.
- After the funeral, if you would like the floral tributes taken to the church we would be happy for that to happen and the funeral director can arrange it for you.

Some words of encouragement and hope from St Paul's Letter to the Romans

I am sure that neither death, nor life … nor things present, nor things to come, nor height, nor depth, nor anything else in all creation, will be able to separate us from the love of God in Christ Jesus our Lord.

Romans 8.38–39

A prayer for personal use

Heavenly Father, giver of all life, I thank you for all the love I have known, and for joys and sorrows shared. Give me the strength I need to give the one I have loved back to you, knowing that they will be safe in your care. And give me the faith I need to trust in your promise of eternal life. Through Jesus Christ our Lord. Amen.

Appendix 2

A Magdalene Ministry

Magdalene Ministry is ministry offered to the bereaved by a team from the church. What is set out below can be adapted according to local circumstances and needs and the availability of helpers.

Why 'Magdalene'? Because Mary Magdalene was there at the death of Christ and was the first to witness to the bereaved disciples that the Lord was risen.

A Magdalene Ministry group

This is a group of people committed to befriending those bereaved people who have contact with the local church.

They meet together regularly after the monthly requiem to review their ministry and plan the annual Eastertide service for the bereaved.

The group undertakes training in whatever skills it feels it needs, such as 'Talking with the recently bereaved' – a training session with a bereavement counsellor.

What the group does:
When a death occurs the minister asks the bereaved whether they would welcome a visit from a member of the group; or a group member calls with a letter from the group offering support now or after the funeral; or a group member sends a letter:

> From St Lucy's Magdalene Group
>
> I was very sorry to hear that you had lost someone near and dear to you. I know our minister is taking the service for you. He will have told you that I would be getting in touch on

behalf of a small group at St Lucy's called the Magdalene Group. We are here to help you in any way we can, either before or after the funeral. For instance, if you need advice, or practical help, or would just like someone to call and chat, please give me a ring, either now or later.

You might also like to know that if the service is in St Lucy's we can tape the address the minister makes and if you would like a copy of it we can let you have one. Just let me know.

Yours sincerely

If the minister is anxious about a bereaved person s/he asks a member of the group to call rather than write.

Members of the group act as stewards at the funeral and sometimes read a lesson or lead prayers.

The group arranges an annual service for those who have been bereaved in the previous twelve months, followed by a simple tea. The group chooses the hymns, prayers and readings and invites a speaker – who may be a minister, or a Christian GP or counsellor. The group sends out the invitations to this:

From St Lucy's Magdalene Group

We are writing to all those who have lost loved ones during the past twelve months and whose funeral services were held at our church or conducted by our minister. We are arranging a special service when we can remember by name your loved one. It will be a short service when we can pray for those we love but see no more; and can ask God to continue to give us the strength we need to face the future.

We shall sing three familiar hymns, have readings and prayer and the minister will give a brief address. Afterwards there will be a cup of tea.

It will be held on Easter Sunday at 3 p.m. The service will last 45 minutes and afterwards you can stay for as long as you like. You will be made most welcome.

With our love

Notes

1 Something happened

[1] *Something Happened* is the title of a book by Joseph Heller, Black Swan, 1972.

[2] The figure for minority ethnic groups is 3.7m (7.1%). However, the minority ethnic population is growing 15 times faster than the white population. Office for National Statistics, *Population Trends*, HMSO, 2001.

[3] Harold Macmillan said, 'Go round the country, go to the industrial towns, go to the farms and you will see a state of prosperity such as we have never had in my life-time – nor indeed ever in the history of this country.' Cited in A. Sampson, *Macmillan: A Study in Ambiguity*. Penguin, London, 1967, p. 159.

[4] Peter Berger uses the phrase in L. Woodhead (ed.) with P. Heelas, and D. Martin, *Peter Berger and the Study of Religion*. Routledge, London, 2001, p. 194.

[5] L. Sage, *Bad Blood: A Memoir*. Fourth Estate, London, 2000, p. 4.

[6] See C. Brown, *The Death of Christian Britain*. Routledge, London, 2001.

[7] This is the thesis of Allan Bloom's *The Closing of the American Mind*. Simon and Schuster, New York, 1987.

[8] P. Berger, 'Protestantism and the quest of certainty', *The Christian Century*, 26 August–2 September 1998, p. 782.

[9] The various titles for religious teaching in schools plots most eloquently the changes I have outlined. Immediately after the Second World War schools taught 'Religious Instruction' (RI) and held a daily act of explicitly Christian worship. Christian faith, based on the Bible, was taught as true. From the 1960s RI became 'Religious Education' (RE) and syllabuses examined the world-wide phenomenon of religion. This relativized all faiths and made it impossible to teach any one as 'true'. Religion was a matter of personal opinion and a matter of subculture. Assemblies became increasingly secular. Finally, religion was subsumed in many schools

in some wider curriculum of social studies. In other words, it was treated as an interesting but minor affair, affecting minority groups among the population.

10 *The Times*, 6 September, 2001.

11 There has been little research into this area and so it is not possible to say whether numbers of people here are particularly significant. Lancaster University Department of Religious Studies has undertaken an extensive study in Kendal that will shed some light, as results become known.

12 'Invictus', by William Ernest Henley (1849–1903). The Oklahoma bomber, Timothy McVeigh, left a handwritten copy of it as his last testament before he was executed in 2001. It was his way of saying he accepted no authority – not even God's – other than his own.

13 This is charted in A. Russell, *The Clerical Profession.* SPCK, London, 1980.

14 During my ministry there have been fashions among the clergy for the kind of socially useful role they have sought to emulate. In the 1960s it was general social work, giving way in the 1970s to a community work model or more active political engagement – I was a local councillor for an inner-city ward for 13 years. By the end of the twentieth century the dominant model was that of the counsellor.

15 Figures from P. Jupp, 'The context of funeral ministry today', in P. Jupp and T. Rogers, *Interpreting Death: Christian Theology and Pastoral Practice.* Cassell, London, 1997, p. 11.

2 What can we say about death?

1 These are the words with which one Dutch theologian begins a work of popular theology. H.M. Kuitert, *I Have My Doubts: How to Become a Christian Without Being a Fundamentalist.* SCM Press, London, 1993. I am indebted to Professor Kuitert's argument on life after death at several points in this chapter.

2 Even in the late nineteenth century family Bibles were being printed which gave the date of creation in marginal notes as 4004 BC. This was the date which James Ussher, Archbishop of Armagh, had worked out in the seventeenth century on the basis of biblical texts.

3 J.-F. Lyotard, *La condition post-moderne.* Minuit, Paris, 1979.

4 W. B. Yeats, 'Death', in *The Chatto Book of Modern Poetry 1915–1955*, eds C. Day Lewis and J. Lehmann. Chatto & Windus, London, 1956, p. 33.

5 M. Foucault, *Discipline and Punish: The Birth of the Prison.* Penguin, London, 1991, p. 304.

6 From the poem by Dylan Thomas, 'Do not go gently into that good night'.
7 John 11; Luke 7.11.
8 The theological answer is somewhat longer! The New Testament generally seems to think that the dead are held in God, or sleep in Christ, until the resurrection.
9 Matthew 22.30.
10 John 20.17.
11 H. Oppenheimer, *Marriage.* Mowbray, London, 1990, p. 114.
12 In his otherwise excellent account of the Christian funeral in *Brief Encounters* (SCM Press, London, 1985), Wesley Carr does not, I think, recognize sufficiently the needs of this group within a funeral congregation.
13 Although New Life charismatic churches use the word 'life' ambiguously – to mean both this life and the next – the focus of their assemblies is the enhancement of the quality of life here and now rather than any concentration on the hereafter.

3. Dying

1 Cited in T. Rennell, *Last Days of Glory: The Death of Queen Victoria.* Viking, London, 2001, p. 144.
2 For an account of Victorian death see J. Stevens Curl, *The Victorian Celebration of Death.* Sutton Publishing, Stroud, 2000. Curl traces the literary influences on the Victorian fascination with death.
3 Rennell, *Last Days,* p. 129.
4 Fortunately the Archbishop was in attendance and was able to pronounce a blessing, finishing at the exact moment Victoria died.
5 The figures are given in P. Jupp, 'The context of funeral ministry today', in P. Jupp and T. Rogers, *Interpreting Death: Christian Theology and Pastoral Practice.* Cassell, London, 1997, p. 11.
6 The most comprehensive survey is in A. Swerdlow, *Cancer Incidence and Mortality in England and Wales: Trends and Risk Factors.* Oxford University Press, Oxford, 2001.
7 See E. Becker, *The Denial of Death.* Free Press, New York, 1973.
8 A. Bennett, *Telling Tales.* BBC, London, 2000, p. 23.
9 The advent of central heating also made it less desirable to keep bodies at home for any length of time.
10 P. Ariès, *The Hour of Our Death.* Allen Lane, London, 1981, p. 560. See also P. Ariès, *Western Attitudes Toward Death: From the Middle Ages to the Present.* Marion Boyars, London, 1974; *Images of Man and Death.* Harvard University Press, Cambridge, Mass., 1985.

[11] Professor Tom Kirkwood, *Brave Old World*. Reith Lecture, 12 April, 2001.

[12] Jupp, 'Context of funeral ministry', p. 11.

[13] The journalist and broadcaster John Diamond wrote a regular column in *The Times* detailing the progress of the throat cancer which eventually killed him. His book is, *C: Because Cowards Get Cancer Too...* Vermilion, London, 1998.

[14] E. Kübler-Ross, *Death: The Final Stage of Growth*, Prentice Hall, London, 1975; *On Death and Dying*, Routledge, London, 1990. Kübler-Ross identifies five 'stages': denial and isolation, anger, bargaining, depression and acceptance. R. Kavanaugh, *Facing Death*, Penguin, London, 1972, suggests seven stages: shock, disorganization, volatile emotions, loss, loneliness, relief and re-establishment.

[15] L. Tolstoy, *Childhood, Boyhood, Youth*. Penguin, London, 1964, pp. 95–6.

4 Death

[1] See for example C. G. Brown, *The Death of Christian Britain*. Routledge, London, 2001.

[2] Karl Rahner speaks of death as putting 'an end to the *whole* man' in his *Theological Investigations*, vol. 4. Darton, Longman & Todd, London, 1966, p. 347. For a medical account of death see S. B. Nuland, *How We Die*. Chatto & Windus, London, 1994.

[3] John 11.25–6.

[4] The final verse of an anthem composed by Arthur Benson for a memorial service at the Royal Mausoleum, Frogmore, on the first anniversary of the death of Queen Victoria. T. Rennell, *Last Days of Glory: The Death of Queen Victoria*. Viking, London, 2001, p. 293.

[5] The hymn is discussed in a book on Victorian hymnody: I. Bradley, *Abide With Me: The World of Victorian Hymns*. SCM Press, London, 1997.

[6] For a summary of attitudes in various traditional societies see P. Ariès, *Western Attitudes Toward Death: From the Middle Ages to the Present*. Marion Boyars, London, 1994. For an account of bereavement in modern Britain see T. Walter, *On Bereavement: The Culture of Grief*. Open University, London, 1999.

[7] Until 1958, half the population died at home. Now only one quarter do. See P. C. Jupp, 'The context of funeral ministry today', in P. C. Jupp and T. Rogers, *Interpreting Death: Christian Theology and Pastoral Practice*. Cassell, London, 1997, p. 6.

[8] The figures are given by Peter Jupp, in 'The context of funeral ministry today', p. 9.

[9] The phrase 'publicly absent but privately present' can be found in P. Mellor, *Death in High Modernity*, in D. Clark (ed.), *The Sociology of Death.* Blackwell, London, 1993.

[10] Psalm 127.4.

[11] The quotations are all from the *Leicester Mercury.*

[12] M. Young and L. Cullen found similar views among East Londoners in their study, *A Good Death: Conversations with East Londoners.* Routledge, London, 1996.

[13] Earl Spencer similarly spoke of his sister, Princess Diana, being 'taken' by God in his oration at the funeral service in Westminster Abbey. This funeral probably suggested to many that funerals could be personalized in more creative ways through the use of more secular music and readings.

[14] Richard Hoggart noted this in *The Uses of Literacy.* Penguin, London, 1957.

[15] The quotation is often unacknowledged but is in fact from Kahlil Gibran, *The Prophet.* Heinemann, London, 1979.

[16] Similar points are made by John Hick, *Death and Immortality.* Collins, London, 1976.

[17] The opening sentence of Nicholas Peter Harvey's book, *Death's Gift: Chapters on Resurrection and bereavement.* Epworth, London, 1985; Eerdmans, Grand Rapids, 1995.

[18] Peter Mullen, *The Spectator*, 27 April 2001.

5 Bereavement

[1] Cited in *The Man from Nazareth As They Saw Him.* Schools Council, 1977, p. 15.

[2] About one in four children died before adulthood at the time of Christ. See R. Radford Ruether, *Christianity and the Modern Family.* SCM London, 2001.

[3] Jeremiah 31.15. 'A voice was heard in Ramah, wailing and loud lamentation, Rachel weeping for her children; she refused to be consoled because they were no more.' Matthew 2.18.

[4] Genesis 3.19.

[5] Psalm 115.17

[6] See Psalm 88.5–6.

[7] 2 Samuel 18.33.

[8] John 11.35.

[9] 1 Thessalonians 4.14.

[10] 1 Thessalonians 4.18.

11 G. Walters, *Why Do Christians Find It Hard To Grieve?* Paternoster Press, Carlisle, 1997.

12 Augustine, *Confessions.* Penguin, London, 1961, pp. 200, 201.

13 Cited in J. Stevens Curl, *The Victorian Celebration of Death.* Sutton Publishing, Stroud, 2000.

14 *The Victorian Celebration of Death*, p. 210.

15 C. S. Lewis, *A Grief Observed.* Faber & Faber, London, 1990.

16 This is the point of citing the Turkish proverb 'He that conceals his grief finds no remedy for it' in a popular clerical handbook first published in the 1980s by Ian Ainsworth and Peter Speck, *Letting Go: Caring for the Dying and Bereaved.* SPCK, London, 1982.

17 M. Foucault, *Discipline and Punish: The Birth of the Prison.* Allen Lane, London, 1977.

18 Cited in T. Walter, *On Bereavement: The Culture of Grief.* Open University Press, Buckingham, 1999.

19 By chance I was in Sheffield visiting Cuddesdon ordinands and so made my way to Hillsborough to help with the bereaved during the late afternoon and through the night. The fact that local churches were all closed on the Saturday afternoon may have been the reason for the initial tying of scarves to the railings: it was a substitute for saying prayers or lighting candles in church. Sheffield Cathedral was the exception and some found their way there.

20 For example: Cruse, The Compassionate Friends, The Stillbirth and Neonatal Deaths Society.

6 Dying well

1 My impression is that nurses have moved ahead more quickly in this respect than doctors.

2 Cited in A. Peberdy, 'Spiritual care of dying people', in D. Dickenson, M. Johnson and J. Samson Katz, *Death, Dying and Bereavement.* Open University Press, Buckingham, 2000, p. 73.

3 *Death, Dying and Bereavement*, p. 74.

4 K. Myers, 'The doctor still can't help you to die well', *Sunday Telegraph*, 18 November 2001.

5 When one examines the amount of resource consumed by practical training in the churches it is astonishing that there is so very little serious evaluation of it. 'Learning outcomes' are rarely examined.

6 See T. Walter, *On Bereavement: The Culture of Grief.* Open University Press, Buckingham, 1999, ch. 11.

7 Cited in J. Hick, *Death and Eternal Life.* Collins, London, 1976, p. 166. Hume died five days later.

[8] S. de Beauvoir, *A Very Easy Death*. Penguin, London, 1983.

[9] The figures are given in C. Seale, 'Demographic change and the experience of dying', in Dickenson et al., *Death, Dying and Bereavement*, p. 35.

[10] John Diamond reported that sadness was his first reaction on being told that his cancer was inoperable. *The Times*, 23 January 1999.

[11] R. McCavery, 'Spiritual care in acute illness' in F. McGilloway and P. Myco (eds), *Nursing and Spiritual Care*. Harper & Row, London, 1985, pp. 129–42.

[12] Ecclesiastes 2.16.

[13] We may find this a shocking idea but it seems to be a not uncommon experience. See P. Houghton, *On Death, Dying and Not Dying*. Jessica Kingsley, London, 2001, p. 101.

[14] See C. Goldberg, *Mourning in Halachah*. Mesorah, New York, 1991.

7 Taking a funeral

[1] The point is well made by Wesley Carr in *Brief Encounters*. SPCK, London, 1985, p. 117.

[2] A printed card could have these elements: the name, address and telephone of the minister; a short message of sympathy and support; a prayer for personal use; a space to record the time and date of the service and any agreed details, such as hymns, music and readings.

[3] A. van Gennep, *The Rites of Passage*. Routledge, London, 1960.

[4] Very similar words to this were used by the Dean of Westminster at the funeral of Princess Diana and were much remarked upon at the time.

8 Good grief

[1] As reflected in Luke 8.51.

[2] Anthony Howard writing in *The Times*, 8 January, 2002. The death of Jennifer Brown was made all the harder for Gordon and Sarah Brown because it was so public. It was also at a time when society was much exercised with other aspects of the care and safety of children. The issue of paedophilia and the murder of Sarah Paynes by a sex-offender also lie behind comments such as this by Libby Purves: 'Grief for a baby is immeasurable, betrayal of a baby the worst crime.' *The Times*, 8 January, 2002. Even so, this assessment of the relative loss of a baby's life, as against, say, the life of a 35-year-old mother of three, seems disproportionate.

[3] J. Morris, *Conundrum*. Oxford University Press, Oxford, 1974.

4 This is still being taught to clergy. For example, in a recent manual the writers say, 'Researchers have observed various stages through which grieving persons need to pass' – though they also speak about the need for the stages to be 'applied flexibly'. F. Watts, R. Nye and S. Savage, *Psychology for Christian Ministry*. Routledge, London, 2002, p. 154.

5 See R. Gross, *Psychology: The Science of Mind and Behaviour*. Hodder & Stoughton, London, 1996.

6 Psalm 73.23, 25.

7 The term is borrowed from Walter Brueggemann, who has some very helpful and insightful comments on those psalms which express deep emotion and anguish. W. Brueggemann, *The Message of the Psalms: A Theological Commentary*. Augsburg, Minneapolis, 1984, pp. 51–121.

8 Trainee counsellors are sometimes referred to William Worden's book, *Grief Counselling and Grief Therapy*, which in the first edition (the position is modified subsequently) speaks of the task of mourning as the withdrawal of emotional energy from the deceased. W. Worden, *Grief Counselling and Grief Therapy*. Routledge, London, 1991.

9 T. Walter, *On Bereavement: The Culture of Grief*. Open University Press, Buckingham, 1999, p. 105.

10 C. M. Parkes and A. Markus (eds), *Coping with Loss*. BMJ Books, London, 1998.

Further reading

A very full bibliography has been produced by the Churches' Group on Funeral Services at Cemeteries and Crematoria, Church House, Great Smith Street, London SW1P 3NZ. The following are books which I have found useful.

Dying

Robbins, J., (ed.), *Caring for the Dying Patient and the Family*. Harper & Row, London, 1989.

Nuland, S. B., *How We Die*. Chatto & Windus, London, 1994.

Hinton, J., *Dying*. Penguin, London, 1972.

Callanan, M. and Kelley, P., *Final Gifts: Understanding and Helping the Dying*. Hodder & Stoughton, London, 1992.

The funeral

Walter, T., *Funerals and How to Improve Them*. Hodder & Stoughton, London, 1990.

Carr, W., *Brief Encounters*. SCM Press, London, 1985.

Bereavement

Murray Parkes, C., *Bereavement – Studies of Grief in Adult Life*. Penguin, London, 1986.

Pincus, L., *Death and the Family*. Faber & Faber, London, 1981.

Manning, D., *Comforting Those Who Grieve*. Collins, London, 1985.

Walter, T., *On Bereavement: The Culture of Grief*. Open University, Buckingham, 1999.

Jacobs, M., *Swift to Hear: Facilitating Skills in Listening and Responding*. SPCK, London, 1986.

Religion in Britain
Brown, C., *The Death of Christian Britain.* Routledge, London, 2001.

Death in history
Ariès, P., *The Hour of Our Death.* Allen Lane, London, 1981.
Ariès, P., *Western Attitudes Toward Death: From the Middle Ages to the Present.* Johns Hopkins University Press, Baltimore, 1974.
Ariès, P., *Images of Man and Death.* Harvard University Press, Cambridge, Mass., 1985.

Theology
Cocksworth, C., *Prayer and the Departed.* Grove Worship Series, Nottingham, 1997.
Hick, J., *Death and Eternal Life.* Macmillan, London, 1985.
Küng, H., *Eternal Life.* Collins, London, 1984.
Jupp, P. and Rogers, T., *Interpreting Death: Christian Theology and Pastoral Practice.* Cassell, London, 1997.

Personal experience
Lewis, C. S., *A Grief Observed.* Faber & Faber, London, 1961.
Diamond, J., C: *Because Cowards Get Cancer Too…* Vermilion, London, 1998.
Houghton, P., *On Death, Dying and Not Dying.* Jessica Kingsley, London, 2001.

For parents and teachers
Jackson, M. and Colwell, J., *A Teacher's Handbook of Death.* Jessica Kingsley, London, 2001.
Holland, J., *Understanding Children's Experiences of Parental Bereavement.* Jessica Kingsley, London, 2001.
Murphy, S., *Coping with Cot Death.* Sheldon, London, 1990.

Music and songs in a time of sorrow
Bell, J. and Maule, G., *When Grief is Raw: Songs for Times of Sorrow and Bereavement.* Wild Goose Publications, Iona Community, Glasgow, 1997.

Index